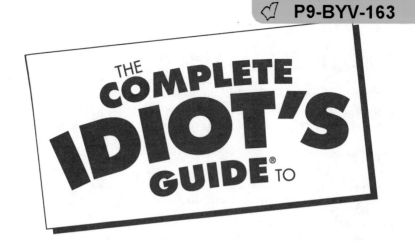

# THE COMPLETE IDIOT'S GUIDE® TO

# Homemade Ice Cream

*by Dick Warren*
*with Bobbi Dempsey*

## ALPHA

A member of Penguin Group (USA) Inc.

*I would like to dedicate this book to my wife, Linda, who has been there to work with me constantly, especially during the most difficult times in my life. Her hard work, extra effort, advice, and tireless dedication have been immense help with this book. Thanks, Linda. With all my love and sincere appreciation.*

*A final note of memoriam to my son Randy, lost to us at age 22. He loved the ice cream business as much as I do and, in my thoughts, will continue to be at my side.*

## ALPHA BOOKS

Published by the Penguin Group

Penguin Group (USA) Inc., 375 Hudson Street, New York, New York 10014, U.S.A.

Penguin Group (Canada), 10 Alcorn Avenue, Toronto, Ontario, Canada M4V 3B2 (a division of Pearson Penguin Canada Inc.)

Penguin Books Ltd, 80 Strand, London WC2R 0RL, England

Penguin Ireland, 25 St Stephen's Green, Dublin 2, Ireland (a division of Penguin Books Ltd)

Penguin Group (Australia), 250 Camberwell Road, Camberwell, Victoria 3124, Australia (a division of Pearson Australia Group Pty Ltd)

Penguin Books India Pvt Ltd, 11 Community Centre, Panchsheel Park, New Delhi—10 017, India

Penguin Group (NZ), cnr Airborne and Rosedale Roads, Albany, Auckland 1310, New Zealand (a division of Pearson New Zealand Ltd)

Penguin Books (South Africa) (Pty) Ltd, 24 Sturdee Avenue, Rosebank, Johannesburg 2196, South Africa

Penguin Books Ltd, Registered Offices: 80 Strand, London WC2R 0RL, England

International Standard Book Number: 1-59257-484-x
Library of Congress Catalog Card Number: 2005937205

08  07  06    8  7  6  5  4  3  2  1

Interpretation of the printing code: The rightmost number of the first series of numbers is the year of the book's printing; the rightmost number of the second series of numbers is the number of the book's printing. For example, a printing code of 06-1 shows that the first printing occurred in 2006.

*Printed in the United States of America*

**Note:** This publication contains the opinions and ideas of its authors. It is intended to provide helpful and informative material on the subject matter covered. It is sold with the understanding that the authors and publisher are not engaged in rendering professional services in the book. If the reader requires personal assistance or advice, a competent professional should be consulted.

The authors and publisher specifically disclaim any responsibility for any liability, loss, or risk, personal or otherwise, which is incurred as a consequence, directly or indirectly, of the use and application of any of the contents of this book.

Most Alpha books are available at special quantity discounts for bulk purchases for sales promotions, premiums, fund-raising, or educational use. Special books, or book excerpts, can also be created to fit specific needs.

For details, write: Special Markets, Alpha Books, 375 Hudson Street, New York, NY 10014.

**Publisher:** *Marie Butler-Knight*
**Editorial Director:** *Mike Sanders*
**Senior Managing Editor:** *Jennifer Bowles*
**Acquisitions Editor:** *Tom Stevens*
**Development Editor:** *Nancy D. Lewis*
**Senior Production Editor:** *Billy Fields*

**Copy Editor:** *Jan Zoya*
**Book Designer:** *Trina Wurst*
**Cover Designer:** *Bill Thomas*
**Indexer:** *Brad Herriman*
**Layout:** *Ayanna Lacey*
**Proofreading:** *John Etchison*

# Contents at a Glance

# Contents

# Foreword

We all know that food nourishes the body. But ice cream, ah yes, ice cream is for the soul. And people take their ice cream very seriously. It conjures up pleasant memories of taking Mom or Dad's or your grandparent's hand and walking down to the corner ice cream store on a warm summer night and enjoying an ice cream cone, or sharing a sundae or banana split with the family. Or as a teenager, going to the local ice cream shop with friends after school or after a dance or football game. Or perhaps you have fond memories of making ice cream in Grandma's kitchen.

No longer reserved for royalty and the very rich, it is an all-American dessert and has been compared to "mom" and "apple pie." And after more than 20 years in the ice cream industry myself, I have never seen anyone eating an ice cream dessert with a frown on their face. Just walk into any ice cream store and watch what happens when the server hands over an ice cream treat, nothing but smiles. Or open up your own freezer and take out the ice cream. Your family will soon be gathered around enjoying a dish of this delicious treat.

Now you can learn how to make the best ice cream, right in your own kitchen, from one of the best in the industry, in simple, easy-to-understand directions, using ingredients found in your local grocery store. With over 50 years of experience in the ice cream industry, Dick Warren will take you on a magical culinary dessert journey in this *Complete Idiot's Guide.* You will quickly learn about the history and folklore surrounding the origins of the dessert and some statistics on just how much ice cream; is eaten in this country every year. Trust me, you'll be amazed at the amount of ice cream we eat. I've heard that there is enough ice cream produced annually in the United States to fill the Grand Canyon!

You'll assemble the equipment and ingredients, and learn how to store your ice cream; then it's on to the fun part. You'll learn basic recipes for mixes and then dozens of recipes for vanilla, chocolate, fresh fruit, and several variations for each category. Then you move on to other flavors like nuts, candy, peanut butter, coffee, honey, margarita, eggnog, and more. Another chapter is devoted to unusual flavors, including vegetables, garlic, mincemeat, molasses, and all types of exotic treats. Sherbet, sorbets, frozen yogurt, and gelato are all explained with dozens more recipes for each category. I couldn't wait to go home and take out my ice cream maker, but there was more.

What ice cream would be complete without toppings? You'll find recipes for chocolate, butterscotch, marshmallow, caramel, fruit based, whipped toppings, and more.

So you've made the ice cream and the toppings; now you'll learn how to "assemble" these components into tasty desserts by making sundaes, banana splits, parfaits, and ice cream sandwiches. You can even make your own cones, ice cream cakes, and pies as well as ice cream sodas, milk shakes, floats, malts, frappes, frosteds, and smoothies, with recipes included for all of these drinks.

As I said, I couldn't wait to take out my ice cream maker and try out several of the recipes. And after many years myself in the ice cream industry, I learned several tips and tricks for making the best ice cream around. I hope you will share your ice cream–making talents in this *Complete Idiot's Guide* with family and friends and make your own pleasant memories.

And if you ever find yourself in Massachusetts, on Cape Cod in the summer, be sure to stop in at Four Seas Ice Cream Store in Centerville for some award-winning and truly legendary ice cream.

Lynda Utterback

**Lynda Utterback** is the Executive Director of the National Ice Cream Retailers Association, the largest trade association for retail ice cream store owners; she is also owner and president of JLM Unlimited, Inc., which produces point-of-sale and training materials for ice cream stores.

# Introduction

Welcome to my world of ice cream. After 50 years in the business, there is no doubt that I still eat, sleep, drink, and even dream ice cream. Even my license plate says "ice cream." I sure hope you will gain ice cream insight and pleasure from this book as you mix up a few interesting flavors in your home.

I was introduced to making ice cream on my grandfather's farm in central Maine at the age of three or four, and at home by my mother, who would bring out the old White Mountain crank freezer at least once a month. When I was 15 and 16, I worked at a girl's camp on the coast of Maine for two summers; and there, the old chef had the four of us maintenance men (boys, actually) cranking out new flavors each Sunday to feed 225 young lady campers. It's no wonder that as a football player at Saugus High, in Massachusetts, I could block with a strong right forearm.

While I was working on my teaching degree at Boston University, the original owner of Four Seas Ice Cream in Centerville on Cape Cod hired me to be an ice cream maker and manager for the summer. Knowing it would be tough to make a living solely as an educator, I took the job, hoping that I could become more involved in the business. In two years I was a partner, and in four years I was the proud and apprehensive owner of the business. That all started in 1956, and although there were tough dues to be paid, I have found that ice cream, and the whole entrepreneur thing, has been good to me. I love meeting and serving people, and I have truly enjoyed dealing in a fun business that contributes to people's happiness.

Along the way, our little shop on Cape Cod has been blessed with numerous awards, accolades, and great recognition by the press. I'll briefly name just a few: *USA Today* newspaper, as one of the top-10 shops in the U.S.A.; *Gourmet* magazine, the best ice cream in New England; *Cape Cod Life* magazine, chosen number one for the past 25 years by its readers; along with mentions in *The New York Times*, *People* magazine, and many more. Probably the best ongoing press has been a PBS show on ice cream, which has continued to air on television for the past 10 years.

In the last few years, I've spent less time at the business, as my son Doug and his wife Peggy are now running the show—but I still work, making ice cream, when needed. When I retired from teaching after 31 years at Barnstable High School, I found more time to do ice cream consulting work and to run seminars. The seminar called "Successful Ice Cream Retailing" has had a great 17-year run, and teaching people the business of ice cream has been a special treat for me.

Okay, enough about what got me to this point, as it's time to talk about the book you are holding in your hands. Experimenting with and making ice cream at home has been quite a change from my small-shop ice cream–making experience. A small ice cream shop owner buys his ice cream basic mix (cream, milk solids, and a stabilizer, etc.) and adds to that his special flavors as they are placed in a five- or ten-gallon batch freezer for manufacturing. These flavorings and other basic ingredients can be purchased from large flavor companies. The exception to that are fresh fruits, if used, and even those are often enhanced with an extract. With home ice cream making, you will need to make flavors that you can purchase at your local grocery store where you can find a large variety of different ingredients. Be creative and experiment.

The chapters begin by covering the very interesting history of ice cream along with other special facts. When you have covered that, it is important to walk you through the proper equipment to use and the best manufacturing procedures. Your process should be fun, not work, and the pride and success in tasting your finished product will hopefully make you want to continue. I have spent a little extra time on the vanilla chapter because vanilla is number one. In 1924, Eddie Cantor sang "I'll Have Vanilla" with his best line stating, "You can shake that milk shake till the cow starts to scream but I'll wait for a plate of vanilla ice cream." Of course, chocolate, which some folks feel is a national addiction, is right in there next. Both vanilla and chocolate are great bases to start your experimentation.

From that starting point, chapters follow on fruit, regular, and unusual flavors. These should prove interesting with many special surprises. You may be amazed at what can make a good flavor, if measured and mixed properly. Some take a little more time to prepare than others but you will find the effort is worth it. No ice cream book would be complete without sherbets and sorbets, which are great and inexpensive summertime treats.

It is also great to experiment with frozen yogurts and gelato—two frozen treats touted by many to be the next big thing in frozen desserts. You'll have to be the judge of that. Along with the yogurt line, one can find and experiment with low-fat and dairy-free recipes. I like the full-fat products but I eat them in moderation.

I also hope and expect that you will have fun making special toppings and creating lots of sundaes, sodas, shakes, and perhaps a banana split. What about a Baked Alaska, an ice cream pie, or cake? Yes, they are all there to try. As you probably know, or at least will soon realize, the use of ice cream is functional in so many different formats. Hopefully, this book will introduce you to many flavors that were previously unknown to you. I sure hope you love them all as much as I have through the years and still crave daily. But remember, take time to have fun, too! Folks often say, "Stop and smell the roses"; well, I even have that flavor for you to try.

I'd like to conclude by saying, "Take it slow and taste the vanilla," another early song title. Enjoy, and thanks for your interest.

## Extras

Look for the little asides and comments I've added throughout the chapters to fill this book with the inside knowledge you need about making homemade ice cream.

### Cool Tips

Extra information not found in the text that will help you in your goal of making delicious homemade ice cream.

### Tasty Terms

Brief explanations of the terminology used in making homemade ice cream.

**The Real Scoop**

Useful, or at least interesting, stuff that enhances your knowledge about ice cream.

**Avoid a Meltdown**

Pitfalls and things to avoid while making homemade ice cream.

# Acknowledgments

Since ice cream at my shop, Four Seas Ice Cream, has been my life for 50 years, I would like to dedicate this book to that special well-known dessert, "ice cream." I would love also to be able to acknowledge all of my faithful customers for their support and encouragement. And thanks especially to every one of my super employees through the years who have become my extended family. They all made such a large contribution in making my ice cream career a real pleasure. There is no doubt, however, that my actual family comes first, especially my wife, Linda. Thanks also to Janice, Douglas, Michael, and Jennifer and their respective families for their support, help, and understanding when it was needed the most.

A special thanks also goes to Dr. Scott Rankin, a special friend who knows more about ice cream than most people would ever hope to know.

Bobbi Dempsey would like to thank Dick Warren and his wife, Linda, for making this project such a fun and educational—not to mention delicious—experience. Also, John, Nick, Brandon, and Jack, plus Marcelle and Tony, and Joe and Bill. Finally, my sister Marylin—and my friends who are like sisters—who, no doubt, will be thinking of me while spending extra hours in the gym to work off all of this ice cream.

## Special Thanks to the Technical Reviewer

*The Complete Idiot's Guide to Homemade Ice Cream* was reviewed by an expert who double-checked the accuracy of what you'll learn here, to help us ensure that this book gives you everything you need to know about ice cream. Special thanks are extended to Scott Rankin.

An avid runner and ice cream consumer (a good combination), Scott A. Rankin earned degrees in Food Science from Brigham Young University (B.S. '91, M.S. '92) and Oregon State University (Ph.D., '96). He is an assistant professor at the University of Wisconsin-Madison, Food Science department, where he administers instructional programs on dairy foods, such as the Premium Ice Cream Project, and conducts research in flavor chemistry. Dr. Rankin is a member of the American Dairy Science Association, the Institute of Food Technologists, and the American Chemical Society. He is married, has five children, and lives in Cross Plains, Wisconsin.

## Trademarks

All terms mentioned in this book that are known to be or are suspected of being trademarks or service marks have been appropriately capitalized. Alpha Books and Penguin Group (USA) Inc. cannot attest to the accuracy of this information. Use of a term in this book should not be regarded as affecting the validity of any trademark or service mark.

# Part 1

# Ice Cream Background

If you've never tried to make your own ice cream, or if you've made a few halfhearted attempts without much success, I'm here to help. In these first few chapters, I'll cover all the important basics to get you started and help you avoid some common pitfalls. I'll discuss all the equipment, supplies, and ingredients you will need in your kitchen before you start. I'll also share some important—and interesting—ice cream facts and tidbits. Once you're ready to get started, I've included some simple recipes that will help you master the basic steps of ice cream making.

# Chapter 1

# A Little Ice Cream History

## In This Chapter

- Ice cream's ancient roots
- Early ice cream in the United States
- Interesting ice cream inventions

It's rare to find anyone who doesn't enjoy ice cream in one form or another. Chances are, you're a fan of ice cream—and you probably even have a favorite flavor. But did you ever stop to wonder how ice cream came to be?

In this chapter, I'll give you the whole scoop on ice cream's early beginnings. I'll also share some interesting facts about this delicious frozen treat.

## Ice Cream's Not-So-Humble Beginnings

Lots of folklore and old wives' tales surround the creation of ice cream and its development through the years. The truth can be a bit, well, slippery—but I'll do my best to help you sort out the truth about ice cream's early years.

When exactly was ice cream invented? It's tough to pinpoint an exact date, but people have been enjoying this delicious treat for thousands of years. There are stories of people in ancient times eating a cold dessert that sounds a lot like ice cream.

Obviously, hundreds or thousands of years ago people didn't have the fancy high-tech freezers you can buy today. So people of ancient times actually ate what you would call a snow cone. These cold treats were made from ice or snow—and, needless to say, needed to be eaten quickly before they melted away.

The International Dairy Foods Association (IDFA) traces the first mentions of ice cream back to the Roman Empire, when Nero Claudius Caesar would send workers to the mountains to fetch snow, which they would then flavor with fruits. A century later, Marco Polo returned from an adventure with a great gift for Italy—a recipe for a treat very similar to what you would now call sherbet or sorbet. Very likely this was a precursor to what the Italians now call *gelato*.

Ice cream (then called cream ice) first started becoming common during the sixteenth and seventeenth centuries in England and France. According to ice cream folklore, Charles I of England ordered that ice cream be served regularly at royal feasts, but demanded that the recipe be kept a closely guarded secret. But once the king was killed, someone on his staff apparently spilled the beans, because the dessert soon caught on among the general population.

**The Real Scoop**

In 1984, President Ronald Reagan designated July as National Ice Cream Month and the third Sunday of the month as National Ice Cream Day.

It didn't take long for ice cream to cross the ocean and become a hit with people of the colonial times in the United States. It really helped when ice houses were first built in the early 1800s. Now there was a way to store frozen treats—no more scooping up snow and frantically eating it before it melted!

However, ice cream remained for a long time an indulgence available only to the wealthy. It was expensive and time-consuming to make— all the ingredients had to be made and mixed by hand through a long, tiring process. Unless you had a crew of servants—or a lot of time to kill—it was unlikely that you would be able to enjoy some ice cream.

New York City—specifically, Chatham Street—can be called the birthplace of the ice cream shop. It was here that the first such shops opened, way back in the late 1700s. According to the IDFA, records kept by a Chatham Street merchant show that President George Washington spent approximately $200 for ice cream during the summer of 1790.

**Cool Tips**

The Library of Congress has preserved an ice cream recipe from Thomas Jefferson's documents. Apparently, the former United States president was fond of vanilla ice cream and he reportedly created this recipe himself. You can see a copy of the recipe at the Library of Congress's website at www. loc.gov/exhibits/treasures/ tri034.html.

In the 1840s, a woman named Nancy Johnson invented a paddle-operated ice cream maker. Soon it was much easier for nonwealthy people to have a taste of this dessert. The first commercial ice cream manufacturer was established in Baltimore, Maryland, in 1851. Jacob Fussell, considered the father of the wholesale ice cream industry, was a milk dealer who wondered what he could do with his surplus cream. His efforts led to the future of commercial ice cream factories. By the late 1800s, soda-fountain shops began cropping up across the country, and ice cream sodas became a huge hit. By the early 1900s, people had already figured out that by combining two or more basic flavors, they could make lots of different blended variations.

If you believe the folklore, the ice cream cone was invented by accident in 1904 during the St. Louis World Exposition. As the story goes, an ice cream salesman ran out of bowls and, thinking quickly, improvised with makeshift containers he made by rolling up waffles he borrowed from a nearby stand. As legend has it, the popsicle was also born around the same time—by a young boy named Frank Epperson, who left a cup of fruit juice outside in the cold overnight with a stirring stick in it. It wasn't until about 20 years later that Epperson patented his edible invention.

During World War II, ice cream was frequently served to United States troops overseas. The soldiers were big fans of ice cream. Unfortunately, people back home couldn't indulge as much as they may have liked—dairy products were rationed during the war. But once the war ended, everyone made up for lost time—ice cream consumption soared in the 1940s.

### The Real Scoop

Since Nancy Johnson first created her paddle ice cream maker, lots of creative inventors have obtained patents for items related to ice cream. From a motorized ice cream cone to a tamper-evident ice cream container—along with countless devices for producing, blending, and serving ice cream—it seems that people never run out of ideas for unique ice cream inventions.

### Tasty Terms

A **novelty** ice cream product is a frozen dessert product made in single-serving sizes and packaged separately. They may or may not actually contain dairy ingredients. Examples of novelty products include fruit bars, ice cream sandwiches, and ice cream cups.

From the 1950s on, the United States enjoyed a tasty trend. The focus was on creating new flavors of ice cream and other types of frozen treats. Soon sherbet came along, followed by frozen yogurt. During the fitness-crazed 1980s, low-fat frozen yogurt was very popular. Following this came many different types of frozen fruit bars, ice cream sandwiches, and other frozen *novelties*.

# Facts and Statistics

Today, ice cream is extremely popular—not to mention profitable. In 2002, total United States sales of ice cream and frozen desserts reached $20.5 billion, according to the IDFA. Of that total, the U.S. spent $8.1 billion on products for "at home" consumption, and spent $12.5 billion on "away from home" frozen-dessert purchases (scoop shops, food-service, and other retail sales outlets).

Statistics compiled by Mintel Market Research Group show that ice cream is enjoying a heyday. The packaged ice cream market grew 17 percent (by dollar figures) from 1999 to 2004. Mintel's figures also show that more than 90 percent of all United States households eat ice cream or related frozen desserts on a regular basis.

When it comes to producing ice cream, the United States is king, leading the world in annual production of ice cream in 2004. More than 9 out of 10 households in the United States eat ice cream frequently. Which state is the ice cream champ? That honor goes to California, which in 2004 produced the most ice cream and related frozen desserts, according to the United States Department of Agriculture. Indiana, Texas, Illinois, Pennsylvania, and Minnesota were also high-volume producers.

According to the United States Department of Agriculture, about 1.6 billion gallons of ice cream and related frozen desserts were produced in 2004 in the United States. That works out to more than 21 quarts per person!

When it comes to ice cream, the United States likes to share the wealth with the rest of the world. The USDA says the United States exported nearly 24,000 metric tons of frozen desserts in 2003—worth about $50 million. The biggest customer? Mexico, which bought around $17 million worth of frozen desserts from the United States.

## The Least You Need to Know

- Ice cream can be traced back thousands of years, to a time when people enjoyed desserts made from ice and snow.
- Royals and the wealthy of England and France enjoyed ice cream with their feasts several centuries ago.
- When ice cream first arrived in the United States, it was a costly dessert available only to the rich.
- A vast majority of United States households eats ice cream on a frequent basis.

# Chapter 2

# What You Must Know About Ice Cream Making

## In This Chapter

- The most important piece of equipment
- Why you may need ice and salt
- Ingredients you'll probably need
- How to store your ice cream products

Before you begin making your delicious ice cream creations, there are some things you must know and do. In this chapter, I'll give some important pointers and outline all the equipment and other supplies you'll need in order to be fully prepared to make the best ice cream possible.

## Choosing Your Equipment

There is one main piece of equipment involved in making ice cream—the ice cream freezer. But you can choose from many different types and models. There is no one "best" type. If you already own an ice cream maker of any type, it's probably perfectly fine. You don't necessarily need to rush out and buy a new one. But for readers who don't already have a machine, I'll describe some of the main characteristics of various types.

It's pretty much just a matter of personal preference. You should also take into consideration your own needs, and how often you plan to actually make ice cream. If you intend to make a lot of ice cream, it would probably be worth it to invest in a pricier top-quality machine. On the other hand, if you're a typical person who plans to whip up only the occasional batch, it wouldn't make much sense to spend a lot of money on equipment.

For clarity purposes, the homemade ice cream machine, in which you make your finished product, often has several names: churn, ice cream maker, ice cream machine. In this book, I will refer to it as the "ice cream freezer," which is not to be confused with the deep freezer where you store your frozen ice cream. Also for clarity purposes, the inside tub of the ice cream freezer, usually made of metal or plastic, where you place the liquid formula will be referred to as the "canister."

# Using an Ice Cream Maker

The main piece of equipment required for making homemade ice cream is an ice cream freezer or churn. There are several different kinds of ice cream freezers. The most common is the bucket freezer, which is the traditional piece of ice cream equipment. It consists of a large bucket with a smaller container that fits inside. Years ago, these buckets were commonly wooden, but today they are usually made of plastic with a steel or tin canister inside.

There's a paddle (known in the ice cream community as a "dasher") that rotates and scrapes the ice cream off the cold walls of the canister. As the dasher blades scrape the frozen ice cream mix off the inside of the canister, it allows the warmer liquid mix

### Avoid a Meltdown

If the dasher of your machine won't turn, it's most likely due to one of several problems. The ice might be jammed, or may not be crushed fine enough. The formula could be frozen to the sides of the canister or may be frozen solid. It may also be that you added the nuts, candies, or other extras too late in the process.

to come in contact with the barrel. The rotation also helps incorporate the much-needed air into the freezing of the product.

## Hand-Cranked Freezers

Some ice cream freezers, especially older models, are operated by turning the crank by hand. This can be time-consuming, not to mention tiring.

When using a hand-cranked ice cream freezer, you will also need crushed ice and rock salt. This is used to chill the product inside while it rotates. I'll go into more detail on using the ice and rock salt in the section titled "Using Ice and Rock Salt" in this chapter.

### Avoid a Meltdown

If this is your first time using your ice cream freezer, be sure you read the directions carefully and thoroughly, and know how to use the machine properly *before* you get out any of the ingredients or begin to attempt making any ice cream. Don't try to "play it by ear" and figure it out as you go along. You'll most likely just end up wasting all the ingredients in your first batch.

## Electric Models

Many new models of ice cream freezers operate with an electric motor. These freezers are more expensive than the hand-cranked types, but I think it's well worth it. It is much easier to make ice cream with an electric machine.

There are numerous types of electric ice cream freezers available. These do not require the use of ice and rock salt. However, they have an inner canister that must spend 24 hours in your home freezer before you use it for a batch of ice cream.

### Cool Tips

Ice cream freezers come in many different sizes, from ½ quart to 10 quarts. The most common type is 4 quarts (1 gallon) for the traditional model, and 1 to 2 quarts for the electric variety.

You can also find a type of electric ice cream freezer that doesn't require pre-freezing. The canister has its own pre-cooling unit built in. This is more expensive, but may be a worthwhile investment if you plan to make a lot of ice cream.

### Cool Tips

You can find many different types of ice cream freezers on eBay and other online markets. You may already have your machine—but if not you can review the more popular and sometimes more expensive choices. You can then make an informed decision on which machine to purchase. In other words, demand and price can help you choose the best equipment.

There are formulas for making ice cream in plastic bags or in a coffee can, but it really doesn't seem worth the effort. Along that line, there is a new ball out (which makes about a pint) by UCO. You add the ingredients to the ball, close it up, and toss it around for about a half-hour, and you are making ice cream. Yes, it's for real.

## Using Ice and Rock Salt

If you are using an ice cream freezer that requires ice and rock salt, you'll need to do some prep work before you can get started. You'll need to get at least 10 or 12 pounds of crushed ice, along with up to 5 cups of rock salt.

Set the covered canister that contains the ice cream mixture in the wooden, metal, or plastic bucket and add about three inches of ice around the canister. (Crushed ice is a necessity here. You can't simply use a big block of ice for this process. The bucket needs to sit in the ice. Being surrounded by ice will keep the bucket cold and allow it to sit upright.) Then start sprinkling the rock salt over the ice that is around the canister. Continue adding layers of ice and rock salt until it reaches the level of the liquid that is inside the canister.

Then put the motor unit in place and plug in the unit (if you are using an electric model). Pay attention! As the ice melts, you will need to add more of the ice and salt mixture. It should take about 20 minutes for the mixture to reach the proper consistency.

If you are using a hand-cranked variety, start cranking. It will probably take about an hour until the mixture reaches the correct ice cream consistency.

### Avoid a Meltdown

When using a hand-cranked or electric ice and rock salt freezer, you will sometimes have to unplug the unit before removing the lid to add ingredients or flavoring. Before removing the lid, make sure to clear away the salt and ice mixture. If any of the salt/ice mixture comes in contact with your batch of ingredients, you will have to throw away the entire batch. When you have finished adding your ingredients, simply plug the freezer back in or resume hand-cranking.

# Blender/Food Processor

You might also find that a blender or food processor can come in handy when making various types of ice cream creations, or for puréeing the fruit mixtures required to make some ice creams, sherbets, and other desserts.

# Other Common Kitchen Supplies

Most of the other things you'll use in making ice cream are common household items that you probably already have in your kitchen—utensils like big spoons, wire whisks, mixing bowls, and an ice cream scooper. You will need lots of containers for storing and refrigerating your recipes. A hand mixer will also come in handy for blending eggs, milk, and other ingredients.

### Avoid a Meltdown

I strongly prefer using stainless-steel mixing bowls. I think you should avoid using glass bowls. The process of making ice cream involves working with mixtures at various temperature extremes, and glass has a tendency to crack or break under these conditions.

# Essential Ingredients to Have on Hand

Obviously, the exact ingredients you'll need will vary depending on the specific recipe. But if you want to be well prepared, there are some common ingredients that are used in many ice cream recipes, so it's good to have these on hand in your kitchen. These include sugar, milk, salt, eggs, heavy and light cream, whipping cream, vanilla extract, and evaporated milk.

# Pre-Cooling Ingredients

When using recipes involving cooked ingredients, use a thermometer to ensure the ingredients are cooled to 40°F before adding it to the ice cream freezer, or refrigerate the recipe overnight.

If you don't have time for that, an alternative is to chill the recipe with an *ice bath*.

**Tasty Terms**

You make an **ice bath** by placing the bowl containing the ice cream mixture into a larger bowl filled with ice and water. Keep the mixture in this bath until it is completely cooled to a temperature of 40°F.

# Sanitation and Storage of Product

As with any type of process involving food, safety and sanitation should be a top priority when making ice cream.

This goes without saying, but you should always make sure that all of your equipment and utensils are clean and in good condition. Washing your utensils with an antibacterial dish detergent is a good idea. Be sure to clean your ice cream freezer well after each use. You should keep ice cream and related desserts at very low temperatures, 0°F to –20°F. Many people eat their ice cream immediately after making it, which of course eliminates the problem of storage. Otherwise, you need to make sure to keep it cold enough.

When it comes to storing ice cream, many products are available today. I have used a variety of items, including paper pints purchased from restaurant wholesalers, and plastic containers that I re-used from other products. Though it might seem obvious, you need ample freezer and refrigerator space when making homemade ice cream. From pre-cooling the ingredients to pre-freezing the bucket to keeping the final product frozen, the process can take up a lot of room. Before you begin, make sure you have ample space in your freezer, or you'll be stuck watching your prized dessert melt away. Modern freezers are frost-free and thus turn on and off at times to defrost, causing a fluctuation of temperature. This will allow some icing or "freezer burn" to the ice cream. If you have a chest freezer, that's a big help. Chest freezers have an added advantage: they usually maintain lower and more steady temperatures than a freezer in a refrigerator.

> **The Real Scoop**
>
> Certain flavors of homemade ice cream tend to become pretty hard when frozen, so some people like to let it sit at room temperature a few moments—allowing it to soften—before eating it. Fruit flavors, which contain a lot of natural water, will freeze harder than just plain vanilla. Sherbet or sorbet that are made with water will also freeze more solid.

## The Least You Need to Know

- An ice cream freezer is the main piece of equipment needed for making homemade ice cream.
- Making ice cream can take time, especially if you use a hand-cranked ice cream freezer, but it can also be very rewarding.
- Aside from the ice cream freezer, most of the other supplies you'll need are likely already in your kitchen.

# Chapter 3

# Ice Cream Recipe Basics

## In This Chapter

- Essential ice cream prerequisites
- Preparing your ice cream freezer for use
- The important ingredients
- Ingredient alternatives and calories

As the old saying goes, you need to walk before you can run. And when it comes to ice cream, you need to learn about the basic ingredients. This chapter will help familiarize you with some basic recipes—before you move on to the fancier varieties.

## Before You Start Freezing

I've gone over the use of ice cream equipment in detail in Chapter 2, but I wanted to reiterate a few important things to note:

- If you are using an electric ice cream freezer, the inner canister needs to be kept in your freezer for 24 hours before you freeze each batch of ice cream. (See your manufacturer's directions.)

⊙ If you use a rock salt freezer, plan on having enough rock salt and crushed ice on hand.

⊙ Have all of your utensils on hand before you start mixing the recipe.

I feel it is important for you to review carefully all of the directions that came with your ice cream freezer before you start the manufacturing process. Now that you've got those important points down, you are ready to learn the basics about making homemade ice cream.

### Cool Tips

Some motors will stop or go very slowly when the ice cream begins to freeze. In other cases, you may need to unplug the machine and open the canister to check on the progress. Before opening the canister, make sure that no ice or rock salt can come in contact with the ice cream—if it does, the batch will be ruined. If the ice cream is not firm enough, plug the machine back in and continue freezing.

# The Technical Aspects of Ice Cream

Good ice cream has great texture and body, but most important, a strong, easy-to-identify flavor. You really should be able to define the base flavor without having to read the name or list of ingredients. For homemade ice cream, a proper balance of fat, water, and sugar is needed, often necessitating some "ongoing adjustments."

The freezing temperature affects the size and structure of ice crystals and thus causes the product to be harder or softer. The amount of sugar will also have an effect, but again, remember that a small home ice cream freezer cannot lower the temperature as fast as the commercial type in an ice cream shop. This is why your product may seem icier, especially after being in your home freezer overnight.

Don't overlook the importance of churning or agitating in the freezing process, as the continual motion prevents lumps. Yes, some air is a good thing in ice cream. In a less-expensive commercial product, however, there can be too much air. Also, rapid freezing and whipping allows for the formation of small ice crystals and helps create a smooth product.

When adding flavoring ingredients, especially alcohol, fruit mixes, and/or chocolate, you alter the freezing process slightly. In the case of alcohol, you may find that if too much is added, the freezing process is almost stopped. That Margarita Ice Cream you made yesterday, even after a night in the freezer, will still be a little soft. But hopefully it will maintain its good flavor. Alcohol and sugar are two ingredients that act like antifreeze in ice cream. In short, the more you add, the more difficult is will be to freeze the product to a desirable consistency.

# The Basic Recipe Ingredients

You can use some very simple ice cream recipes as they are, or use them as the foundation for other fancier recipes. These recipes use a few simple ingredients—mainly eggs, cream, milk, and sugar. Each ingredient plays an important role in the final product, and by adjusting the amounts and ratio of these ingredients, you can change the texture, consistency, and flavor of the ice cream.

## Eggs

Eggs are kind of like the glue that holds the ice cream together. They help keep the mixture thick and also aid in blending the other ingredients together. Eggs and egg products are also used to enhance frozen custard product. The USDA recommends (and so do I) that you cook your egg mixtures until they reach 160°F. This heating practice should be employed any time you are using a raw ingredient, such as eggs, that may contain disease-causing bacteria.

## Milk and Cream

Milk and cream are essential ingredients that make your product rich and, well, creamy. The milkfat found in milk and cream provides the flavor and richness of the final product. The key is finding the right proportion of milk and cream. If you use low-fat milk, for example, you'll need more cream in order to achieve the consistency most people find desirable.

The U.S. federal government requires that ice cream mixes contain at least 10 percent milkfat to meet the legal standard of identity. Some super-premium ice creams contain 18 to 20 percent milkfat, reflective of a rich and indulgent product. Manufacturing ice cream at home, you are typically limited to using milk and cream products that are readily available in the store.

Because milkfat is so important in ice cream, what follows are some descriptions of milk and cream products you will encounter and their respective milkfat percentages, as defined by the International Dairy Foods Association:

- Milk—contains no less than 3.25 percent milkfat.
- Half-and-half—mixture of milk and cream containing between 10.5 percent and 18 percent milkfat.
- Light cream—contains between 18 percent and 30 percent milkfat.
- Light whipping cream—also known as just whipping cream, this contains between 30 and 36 percent milkfat.
- Heavy cream—contains at least 36 percent milkfat.
- Evaporated milk—made by removing about 60 percent of milk's water, this is a heat-sterilized product with a longer shelf life. It contains between 6.5 percent and 16.5 percent milkfat.

## Sugar

Sugar (or another sweetener) obviously makes the ice cream taste sweet, but it also serves another significant purpose: freezing point depression. Most typical ice creams, even just coming out of your chest freezer, are still "scoopable" in spite of being at around 0°F.

Remember from your high school chemistry class that water freezes at 32°F? So why isn't ice cream as hard as a rock at 0°F? Because of sugar. Sugar, referring to cane sugar or sucrose, lowers the freezing point of the ice cream mix. The more sugar you dissolve into the ice cream mix, the lower the freezing point. This phenomenon has a chemical basis so if you choose a sweetener that is chemically different than sucrose, such as honey or a non-caloric sweetener, the freezing point may be dramatically different. The results may yield an ice cream that is hard as a rock in one extreme, or may not freeze at all in the other extreme.

For you science fair aficionados, this phenomenon is one of several colligative properties of matter, if you really want the nitty gritty details. But when you alter the sugar content, look out!

# The Basic Recipes

The mixes that follow have no flavorings added to them. What I have tried to do is give you base mixes using different formulas for creating your own flavors. When you add, let's say, an almond extract to any of the basic mixes that follow, you will be making almond ice cream.

In the chapters that follow, I will give you specific formulas with ingredient amounts for each flavor.

## Basic Mix #1

1¼ cups sugar

3 cups heavy cream

3 cups light cream

**Yield:** 2 quarts

**Prep time:** 10 minutes

**Cook time:** None

1. In a mixing bowl, whisk sugar with heavy cream and light cream until dissolved.

2. Cool mixture to 40°F in your refrigerator.

3. Transfer cold formula into the ice cream freezer and freeze according to manufacturer's instructions.

# Basic Mix #2

4 eggs

2 cups half-and-half

1¾ cups sugar

2 cups heavy cream

| **Yield:** 2 quarts |
| **Prep time:** 15 minutes |
| **Cook time:** 8 minutes |

1. Beat eggs and sugar until light and fluffy.

2. In a heavy saucepan, add beaten eggs mixture to 2 cups of half-and-half. Over medium heat, stir constantly until mixture thickens and reaches 160°F (coats spoon).

3. Add remaining heavy cream and mix well.

4. Cool mixture to 40°F in your refrigerator.

5. Transfer cold formula into the ice cream freezer and freeze according to manufacturer's instructions.

# Basic Mix #3

3 cups whipping cream

1 cup whole milk

2 cups sweetened condensed milk (cold)

| **Yield:** 2 quarts |
| **Prep time:** 10 minutes |
| **Cook time:** None |

1. Whisk whipping cream, whole milk, and condensed milk together until well blended.

2. Cool mixture to 40°F in your refrigerator.

3. Transfer cold formula into the ice cream freezer and freeze according to manufacturer's instructions.

# Low-Sugar/Low-Fat/Low-Carb Ingredient Alternatives

As you've probably noticed, ice cream recipes tend to be high in sugar and/or fat. But options are indeed available if you wish to adapt your ice cream recipes to your low-sugar, low-fat, or low-carb lifestyle. Here are some examples you might want to consider:

- Low- or no-sugar: Many sugar-free substitute sweeteners are available today. Some popular examples include Equal, Nutra-Sweet, and Splenda. These have very few (if any) calories. However, some people feel that they don't work as well as good old-fashioned sugar, and that they taste different. If you don't want to use actual sugar, then experiment with some of these substitutes and see which you prefer. Keep in mind that it's impossible to make ice cream without some form of sugar or sweetener. Substitute sweeteners contain few, if any, calories, but you may sacrifice quality.

- Low-fat: The best way to reduce the fat content in ice cream is by adjusting the type of milk and/or cream you use. Substitute skim milk for whole milk, and use light cream whenever possible. Here again, you may sacrifice the quality and flavor.

- Low-carbohydrate: Unfortunately, it's tough to make a truly low-carb ice cream recipe. You can lower the carbohydrate count by watching the mix-in's you use. Even seemingly "healthy" stuff like fruit can really affect the carbohydrate content. Tropical fruits tend to be higher in carbohydrates—so if you use fruit in your ice cream, strawberries are a better low-carb option than bananas or pineapples.

To help you with some of your low-sugar, low-fat, and low-carb choices, the following is a calorie-counter chart for the most common ice cream ingredients.

**The Real Scoop**

Each ½ cup of vanilla ice cream contains approximately 250 calories; light vanilla contains around 100 calories.

**Milk**

> Skim, 1 cup = 80 calories
>
> 1% fat, 1 cup = 100 calories
>
> 2% fat, 1 cup = 120 calories
>
> Whole, 1 cup = 150 calories

**Cream**

> Whipping cream (heavy), 1 TB. = 50 calories
>
> Light cream, 1 TB. = 30 calories
>
> Half-and-half – 1 TB. = 20 calories

**Chocolate**

> Chocolate chips, ½ cup = 400 calories
>
> Semisweet baking squares, 1 ounce = 140 calories
>
> Unsweetened baking squares, 1 ounce = 140 calories

**Yogurt**

> Whole-milk yogurt, 1 cup = 150 calories
>
> Low-fat yogurt, 1 cup = 135 calories

**Strawberries**

> ½ cup (fresh) = 14 calories

**Bananas**

> 1 banana = 100 calories

**Blueberries**

> 1 cup (fresh) = 80 calories

This is meant to serve only as a general guideline. Caloric content can vary from one brand or product to another, so it's best to check the specific labels whenever possible.

# Part 2

# Ice Creams with Flavor

Now that you've mastered the basics, you're ready to add some flavor to the equation. I start out with the most popular flavor, vanilla. And it seems only natural to follow that up with chocolate. From there, I guide you through an assortment of fruit flavors and other common varieties. For those who hunger for something different, I've also included plenty of unusual flavors. Trust me, there's enough variety here to satisfy even the most adventurous ice cream lover.

# Chapter 4

# Vanilla Recipes

## In This Chapter:

- ○ Why vanilla is so costly
- ○ Vanilla recipes, from simple to fancy
- ○ How to spot a good vanilla bean

Vanilla is often called the "king of flavors" when it comes to ice cream, because it is by far the most popular. In the United States, vanilla remains the top-selling flavor by a considerable margin. That's true worldwide, with only a few countries reporting another flavor (usually chocolate) as the top seller.

In this chapter, I'll tell you how vanilla was created and what makes it so special.

## Facts About Vanilla

People have been enjoying the flavor of vanilla for hundreds of years. It probably originated somewhere near the Gulf of Mexico where people of Mesoamerican times—most likely the Aztecs—began cultivating it. Vanilla is the bean of a special orchid plant. Although there are over 55 different species of vanilla orchids,

### The Real Scoop

A lot of the vanilla imported today is from Madagascar. Vanilla is also cultivated in many other countries including Tahiti and Mexico. To the discerning palate, vanilla from each of these countries varies in flavor character. The climate, species grown, and cultivation and production practices specific to the region create the flavor character of the vanilla bean.

### Avoid a Meltdown

Vanilla beans are often sold in small plastic containers. The beans should be a shiny dark color, and should be plump and moist. If the beans are hard or dry and shriveled, it means they are too old.

most vanilla used today is derived from one of two specific types of orchids.

Although it is often underappreciated and overlooked in the wake of fancier flavors, vanilla is a wonderful flavor that has withstood the test of time. It has an extremely rich and creamy taste that many people really enjoy. Whenever possible, you should always use pure, natural vanilla extract. Artificial or synthetic vanilla preparations can often have a bitter taste, and do not have the full taste of natural vanilla.

For some of the recipes in this chapter, you will need vanilla pods or beans. (The two terms are generally used interchangeably to refer to the long, thin capsule that contains lots of little seeds.)

You can buy these at many large grocery stores, health food stores, and lots of online grocery websites.

## Pure vs. Artificial

Read labels carefully when buying vanilla products. The Food and Drug Administration has strict rules concerning the use of the term "vanilla." If a product is labeled "vanilla ice cream," it must contain pure vanilla extract. If the product is made from mostly pure vanilla— along with other flavor ingredients—it must be called "vanilla flavored." If it is mostly or totally made from artificial flavorings, the label must specify "artificial vanilla."

Pure vanilla is more expensive than the artificially flavored variety. I've used both with good results. There may be some regional preferences, though. In certain parts of the country, people expect pure vanilla and are accustomed to that taste.

# Easy Vanilla Ice Cream

3 cups half-and-half

1 cup sugar

3 cups whipping cream

2 tsp. vanilla extract

**Yield:** About 2 quarts

**Prep time:** 15 minutes

**Cook time:** None

1. Mix half-and-half with sugar and beat until sugar is dissolved.

2. Add whipping cream and vanilla and mix well.

3. Cool mixture to 40°F in your refrigerator.

4. Transfer formula into the ice cream freezer and freeze according to manufacturer's instructions.

## The Real Scoop

According to Guinness World Records, the record for eating the most ice cream in 30 seconds using a teaspoon was set by America's Diego Siu, who ate 264 grams (9.3 ounces) at the Central Florida Fair, Orlando, Florida, U.S., on March 2, 2003.

Guinness World Record rules insist that the ice cream—which must be a standard vanilla flavor—is removed from the freezer five minutes before the attempt begins, and that it is eaten straight from the container using just one teaspoon in one hand.

# Simple Vanilla Ice Cream

5½ cups heavy cream

1¼ cups sugar

2 tsp. vanilla extract

| | |
|---|---|
| **Yield:** About 2 quarts | |
| **Prep time:** 15 minutes | |
| **Cook time:** None | |

1. Mix the heavy cream, sugar, and vanilla extract together until well blended.

2. Cool mixture to 40°F in your refrigerator.

3. Transfer cold formula into the ice cream freezer and freeze according to manufacturer's instructions.

 **The Real Scoop**

People in the United States really love vanilla. The country uses more than half of all vanilla beans produced each year.

# Vanilla Bean Ice Cream

2 vanilla beans

3 cups light cream

1 ½ cups sugar

1 TB. vanilla (optional)

2 cups half-and-half

1 cup heavy cream

| **Yield:** 2 quarts |
| --- |
| **Prep time:** 1 hour |
| **Cook time:** 15 minutes |

1. Split vanilla beans down the middle, and with a sharp knife scrape out seeds.

2. In a heavy saucepan over medium heat, add light cream, sugar, vanilla seeds, and pods. The longer the pods sit, the more concentrated the flavor will be.

3. Heat while stirring constantly until bubbles form around edge of saucepan (soft boil). Remove from heat and allow to cool in an ice bath.

4. Remove seed pods (you can use a coffee grinder or food processor to grind pods very fine and add back to mixture).

5. Add half-and-half and heavy cream, and mix well.

6. Cool mixture to 40°F in your refrigerator.

7. Transfer cold formula into the ice cream freezer and freeze according to manufacturer's instructions.

# Mom's Vanilla Ice Cream

4 egg yolks

1 cup sugar

2 cups light cream

2 cups whipping cream

1 cup light corn syrup

1 TB. vanilla extract

| **Yield:** About 2 quarts |
|---|
| **Prep time:** 35 minutes |
| **Cook time:** 15 minutes |

1. Beat egg yolks until light and frothy, add sugar, and beat well.

2. In a double boiler or heavy saucepan over medium heat, cook egg yolks, sugar, and 2 cups light cream. When mixture reaches 160°F, remove from heat and add whipping cream, corn syrup, and vanilla extract. Mix well.

3. Cool mixture to 40°F in your refrigerator.

4. Transfer cold formula into the ice cream freezer and freeze according to manufacturer's instructions.

# Vanilla Chocolate Chip Ice Cream

2 cups whipping cream

1 cup milk

2 cups light cream

2 TB. vanilla

1½ cups sweet chocolate bits (you can add more)

| **Yield:** 2 quarts |
|---|
| **Prep time:** 10 minutes |
| **Cook time:** None |

1. Mix whipping cream, milk, light cream, and vanilla together.

2. Cool mixture to 40°F in your refrigerator.

3. Transfer cold formula into the ice cream freezer and freeze according to manufacturer's instructions.

4. When ice cream is almost frozen, add in chocolate bits. (Or you can add bits quickly after freezing is done.)

## Sweet Vanilla Ice Cream

3 cups light cream

1 cup whipping cream

2 cups sweetened condensed milk

3 tsp. vanilla extract

**Yield:** About 2 quarts

**Prep time:** 15 minutes

**Cook time:** None

1. Mix light cream, whipping cream, condensed milk, and vanilla extract together, and blend until well incorporated.

2. Cool mixture to 40°F in your refrigerator.

3. Transfer cold formula into the ice cream freezer and freeze according to manufacturer's instructions.

## Philadelphia Vanilla Ice Cream

3 cups heavy cream

3 cups light cream

1¼ cups sugar

2 tsp. vanilla extract

**Yield:** About 2 quarts

**Prep time:** 15 minutes

**Cook time:** None

1. Mix heavy cream, light cream, sugar, and vanilla extract together until well blended.

2. Cool mixture to 40°F in your refrigerator.

3. Transfer cold formula into the ice cream freezer and freeze according to manufacturer's instructions.

 **Cool Tips**

Philadelphia-style vanilla is typically recognized for having vanilla bean seed specks in it.

# Marshmallow Vanilla Ice Cream

10 large marshmallows
(4½ ounces in mini marshmallows)

1 cup milk

¾ cup table sugar

2 cups half-and-half

2 cups light cream

1 TB. vanilla extract

**Yield:** About 2 quarts

**Prep time:** 10 minutes

**Cook time:** 10 minutes

1. In a heavy saucepan, mix marshmallows, milk, and sugar. Cook over low heat until marshmallows are dissolved (about 10 minutes).

2. Remove from heat and add the half-and-half, light cream, and vanilla extract. Mix until well blended.

3. Cool mixture to 40°F in your refrigerator.

4. Transfer cold formula into the ice cream freezer and freeze according to manufacturer's instructions.

# Old-Fashioned Vanilla Ice Cream

1 TB. gelatin (unflavored)

5 cups heavy cream

1½ cups table sugar

1 cup evaporated milk

2 tsp. vanilla extract

**Yield:** About 2 quarts

**Prep time:** 15 minutes

**Cook time:** 20 minutes

1. Add gelatin to 1 cup heavy cream and let stand 10 minutes.

2. In a heavy saucepan, heat 2 cups heavy cream to a soft boil (bubbling just around edge of pan).

3. Remove from heat and add gelatin mixture. Mix well.

4. Add sugar and mix until sugar is dissolved.

5. Add remaining heavy cream and evaporated milk, and mix well.

6. Cool mixture to 40°F in your refrigerator.

7. Transfer cold formula into the ice cream freezer and freeze according to manufacturer's instructions.

# Cherry Vanilla Ice Cream

1 (8-oz.) jar maraschino cherries (juice reserved)

2 cups whipping cream

2 cups heavy cream

1 cup milk

2 TB. vanilla extract

**Yield:** 2 quarts

**Prep time:** 10 minutes

**Cook time:** None

1. Cut cherries in halves or quarters. Reserve the juice.

2. Mix cherry juice, whipping cream, heavy cream, milk, and vanilla until well blended.

3. Cool mixture to 40°F in your refrigerator.

4. Transfer cold formula into the ice cream freezer and freeze according to manufacturer's instructions.

5. When ice cream is almost ready to be taken from freezer, add in cherries. (Or you can add cherries quickly after freezing is done.)

# French Vanilla Ice Cream

5 egg yolks

2 cups half-and-half

1⅓ cups table sugar

2 cups heavy cream

2 tsp. vanilla extract

| **Yield:** About 2 quarts |
| **Prep time:** 35 minutes |
| **Cook time:** 15 minutes |

1. Beat egg yolks and sugar until light and fluffy.

2. In a double boiler over medium heat, add half-and-half and egg mixture. Stir constantly until temperature reaches 160°F or until mixture coats back of spoon. Do not boil.

3. Remove from heat, add heavy cream and vanilla. Mix well.

4. Place a piece of plastic wrap over top of mixture to keep a skin from forming.

5. Cool mixture to 40°F in your refrigerator.

6. Transfer cold formula into ice cream freezer and freeze according to manufacturer's instructions.

 **The Real Scoop**

The USDA recommends that you cook this mixture to 160°F. This heating practice should be employed any time you are using a raw ingredient, such as eggs, that may contain disease-causing bacteria.

**Variations:**

*Vanilla with Chips:* peanut butter, butterscotch, chocolate, or caramel. Stir these into ice cream quickly after removing dasher from freezer.

*Vanilla with Ripples* (Swirl): flavors include chocolate syrup, chocolate fudge topping, caramel, butterscotch, raspberry, strawberry, peanut butter, and marshmallow.

The easiest way to ripple your ice cream is to remove the dasher from the finished frozen product. Make a hole in the center of the ice cream, with the handle of a spatula or with anything long enough to reach the bottom. Now pour the ripple ingredients into the hole. Follow that procedure by making a double or triple cross-effect with a knife, which moves the ripple from the middle to the edge of the container. Then scoop the product into pint or quart containers and place in the freezer.

You can also ripple by putting a small amount of ice cream in a container and then adding a little of the ripple ingredient and slowly stirring it in. Repeat this until the container is full.

*Vanilla with Candies:* pecan pralines, chocolate-coated ginger, chocolate-covered cranberries, any crushed candy bar, M&Ms. Stir into ice cream quickly after removing dasher from freezer.

*Vanilla with Baked Goods:* pie crust, brownies, any type of cookie, even cookie dough.

Make sure to chop the ingredients small enough to quickly stir into the ice cream after the dasher is removed.

### The Real Scoop

You can combine any of the above ingredients, but use your imagination and I'm sure you can come up with several ideas of your own. Have fun making up a name for your new flavor.

For example, you can make up a kid's flavor and call it "Gummy Bear Pillows." Just add small gummy bear candies and some miniature marshmallows to any of the vanilla recipes. A little pink food coloring will make it pleasing to their eyes.

# Vanilla Pudding Ice Cream

2 egg yokes

1 cup table sugar

2 pkg. instant vanilla pudding (3¾ oz. each)

4 cups whole milk

2 cups half-and-half

**Yield:** About 2 quarts

**Prep time:** 40 minutes

**Cook time:** 20 minutes

1. Beat eggs and sugar until mixture is creamy.

2. In a double boiler or heavy saucepan add 2 cups milk, heat until milk is hot. (DO NOT BOIL.)

3. Remove from heat and very slowly add hot milk to the creamed egg mixture so as not to cook the eggs.

4. Return mixture to clean double boiler or heavy saucepan and cook over medium low heat until mixture reaches 160°F.

5. Remove from heat and place in an ice bath until cold to the touch.

6. In a mixing bowl combine remaining 2 cups milk with half-and-half. Slowly add instant pudding and whisk until totally dissolved and smooth (no lumps).

7. When pudding is totally incorporated add the cold egg mixture and blend well.

8. Cool to 40°F.

9. Freeze mixture in your ice cream maker according to manufacturer's instructions.

**5**

# Chocolate Recipes

## In This Chapter

- How chocolate is made
- Does chocolate get a bad rap?
- Factors that affect chocolate's taste

Vanilla may be the king of ice cream flavors, but chocolate is a strong second-place favorite. It's hard to find anyone who doesn't like chocolate. In fact, many people find it tough to imagine life without this delicious flavor.

## Where Chocolate Comes From

In an ideal world, chocolate bars would grow on trees (and while we're at it, they'd have zero calories, too). But unfortunately that's not really the case. However, chocolate does essentially come from a tree.

The cocoa tree, which can be found in Brazil, Indonesia, and other parts of the world, produces pods that contain cocoa beans. The beans are fermented, during which their rich flavor intensifies. The beans are then taken to a chocolate factory, where they are roasted and their shells are removed. The inside

of the bean is then made into a liquid. When the liquid is mixed with other ingredients such as milk or cocoa butter, it eventually becomes a candy bar. It can also be ground to make cocoa powder.

# Is Chocolate Bad for You?

You almost have to feel sorry for chocolate. Despite making people's lives a little sweeter, chocolate has been blamed for everything from obesity to bad teeth. We've even heard that chocolate will cause your face to break out. At the same time, some people consider chocolate to be an aphrodisiac or an antidepressant. So what's the real skinny on chocolate? Well, it depends on who you ask. But I think eating chocolate in moderation is fine. True, chocolate does contain saturated fat, which isn't great for your heart. But I've heard of some studies that showed that other ingredients in chocolate are actually *good* for your heart.

> **The Real Scoop**
>
> It's not easy to satisfy America's chocolate craving. Every day, the United States manufactures 3.5 million pounds of chocolate just to make chocolate ice cream, according to the Chocolate Manufacturers Association.

I certainly wouldn't recommend eating a case of chocolate bars every day. But if your overall diet is nutritious and healthy, I think an occasional chocolate snack is not only okay, it's also a well-deserved treat.

# How Chocolate Tastes

As anyone who has tasted a lot of chocolate can tell you, there are many different varieties. Obviously, there is milk chocolate and dark chocolate, but even under the generic label of "chocolate" there are lots of variations. The specific taste will depend on several factors, starting with the bean itself. A bean crop from one part of the world will have its own unique taste, which will be totally different from a crop gathered elsewhere. The taste is also affected by how the beans are fermented and roasted in the factory. Depending on how long they are roasted, or how hot and humid the environment is, the taste will change.

Also, most of the taste variations in chocolate candy are due to the ingredients that have been mixed with the cocoa. Cocoa beans themselves don't taste that great, so they are mixed with other ingredients like milk, butter, and sugar. By tinkering with the ratio of these added ingredients, you will change the taste of the final product.

**Cool Tips**

The scientific name for chocolate is *theobroma cacao*, which translates as "food of the gods." So I suppose it's only natural to describe the taste of chocolate as heavenly!

# Chocolate Facts

Chocolate is big business in the United States. According to the Chocolate Manufacturers Association (CMA), the retail chocolate industry in the United States is worth $13 billion per year. The CMA also says that 65 percent of American chocolate eaters prefer milk chocolate. But we are not selfish when it comes to our beloved flavor. In 2002 the industry exported more than $726 million in chocolate and related products to more than 50 countries around the world.

**The Real Scoop**

Extra-bittersweet, bittersweet, and semisweet are all varieties of dark chocolate. The only difference is the amount of sugar each contains.

# Chocolate Ice Cream

4 squares unsweetened chocolate

3 cups half-and-half

3 cups heavy cream

1¼ cup sugar

1 TB. vanilla extract

Pinch of salt

**Yield:** About 2 quarts

**Prep time:** 20 minutes

**Cook time:** 10 minutes

1. Melt grated chocolate squares in top of double boiler over low heat (simmering water). Do not boil. Add 1 cup light cream very slowly to chocolate mixture. Mix until smooth and creamy. Remove from heat.

2. Mix the rest of light cream, heavy cream, sugar, vanilla, and salt together until sugar is dissolved. Add melted chocolate mixture and mix.

3. Cool mixture to 40°F in your refrigerator.

4. Transfer cold formula into the ice cream freezer and freeze according to manufacturer's instructions.

# Rich Chocolate Ice Cream

6 squares unsweetened chocolate

3 cups heavy cream

3 cups light cream

2 cups table sugar

1 tsp. vanilla extract

| **Yield:** About 2 quarts |
|---|
| **Prep time:** 20 minutes |
| **Cook time:** 10 minutes |

1. Melt grated chocolate squares in top of double boiler over low heat (simmering water). Do not boil. Stir constantly until smooth and creamy. Remove from heat.

2. Add 1 cup light cream very slowly to melted chocolate squares. Blend until smooth and creamy. Remove from heat.

3. In a large bowl add light cream, heavy cream, sugar, and vanilla. Mix until sugar is dissolved. Add chocolate mixture and mix until smooth.

4. Cool mixture to 40°F in your refrigerator.

5. Transfer cold formula into the ice cream freezer and freeze according to manufacturer's instructions.

# Sweet Chocolate Ice Cream

4 squares unsweetened chocolate

3 cups whipping cream

2 cups unsweetened condensed milk (cold)

1¼ cups table sugar

1 TB. vanilla extract

**Yield:** About 2 quarts

**Prep time:** 20 minutes

**Cook time:** 10 minutes

1. Melt grated chocolate in top of double boiler over low heat (simmering water) until smooth and creamy. Do not boil. Remove from heat.

2. Add 1 cup whipping cream very slowly to chocolate squares and mix until smooth and creamy.

3. In a large bowl mix whipping cream, unsweetened condensed milk, vanilla, and sugar until sugar is dissolved.

4. Add chocolate mixture to cream mixture and mix well.

5. Cool mixture to 40°F in your refrigerator.

6. Transfer cold formula into the ice cream freezer and freeze according to manufacturer's instructions.

# Light Chocolate Ice Cream

2 egg yolks

2 cups light cream

1 cup sugar

1 cup chocolate syrup

2 cups whipping cream

1½ TB. vanilla extract

**Yield:** About 2 quarts

**Prep time:** 25 minutes

**Cook time:** 10 minutes

1. Beat egg yolks and sugar until light and fluffy.

2. In top of double boiler over low heat add egg mixture and 2 cups light cream. Stir constantly until mixture reaches 160°F and coats the back of a spoon. Do not boil.

3. Remove from heat.

4. In a large bowl combine chocolate syrup, whipping cream, and vanilla, and mix well. Add egg mixture and mix until combined.

5. Cool mixture to 40°F in your refrigerator.

6. Transfer cold formula into the ice cream freezer and freeze according to manufacturer's instructions.

# Dark Chocolate Ice Cream

5 oz. unsweetened chocolate

1 cup milk

1 envelope unflavored gelatin
(1 TB.)

2 cups whipping cream

2 cups half-and-half

2 cups sugar

2 TB. vanilla extract

**Yield:** About 2 quarts

**Prep time:** 20 minutes

**Cook time:** 10 minutes

1. In top of double boiler over low heat (simmering water) melt grated unsweetened chocolate. Do not boil. Remove from heat.

2. Slowly add 2 cups of half-and-half and blend until smooth and creamy.

3. Add gelatin to 1 cup of milk and allow to sit for 10 minutes or until gelatin is completely dehydrated.

4. In a large bowl add the melted chocolate, whipping cream, gelatin, sugar, and vanilla. Mix well.

5. Cool mixture to 40°F in your refrigerator.

6. Transfer cold formula into the ice cream freezer and freeze according to manufacturer's instructions.

# Chocolate Rum Raisin Ice Cream

3 oz. semisweet chocolate

3 cups light cream

2 cups heavy cream

1 cup table sugar

1 cup raisins

3 TB. rum flavoring (or to taste)

| **Yield:** About 2 quarts |
| --- |
| **Prep time:** 20 minutes |
| **Cook time:** 10 minutes |

1. In the top of a double boiler over low heat (simmering water) melt semisweet chocolate. Remove from heat.

2. To melted chocolate, slowly add 1 cup light cream. Mix until combined.

3. In a mixing bowl add remaining light cream, heavy cream, sugar, and rum flavoring. Beat until sugar is dissolved.

4. Add chocolate mixture and blend well.

5. Cool mixture to 40°F in your refrigerator.

6. Transfer cold mixture to the ice cream freezer and follow manufacturer's guidelines.

7. Just before removing ice cream from ice cream freezer, add in raisins.

### Cool Tips

You can use ½ cup of rum liquor to soak the raisins for a half hour. For a stronger flavor, use more of the rum flavoring.

# Chocolate Spice Ice Cream

3 oz. unsweetened chocolate

1 cup whole milk

2 cups whipping cream

2 cups half-and-half

1½ cups table sugar

1 TB. vanilla extract

4 TB. cinnamon

**Yield:** About 2 quarts

**Prep time:** 20 minutes

**Cook time:** 10 minutes

1. In a double boiler over low heat (simmering water) melt grated unsweetened chocolate. When melted, slowly stir in milk until smooth and creamy. Remove from heat.

2. Mix sugar with cinnamon, as it will incorporate better with the liquid.

3. In a mixing bowl combine whipping cream, half-and-half, sugar/cinnamon mixture, and vanilla extract. Blend until sugar is dissolved.

4. Add chocolate liquid and incorporate well.

5. Cool mixture to 40°F in your refrigerator.

6. Transfer cold mixture to the ice cream freezer and follow manufacturer's guidelines.

# Chocolate Peanut Butter Ice Cream

4 oz. unsweetened chocolate

2 TB. cocoa powder

3 egg yolks

2½ cups whole milk

3 cups whipping cream

1½ cups table sugar

1 TB. vanilla extract

1¼ cups smooth peanut butter

**Yield:** About 2 quarts

**Prep time:** 30 minutes

**Cook time:** 15 minutes

1. Mix cocoa powder with ½ cup sugar.

2. In a double boiler over low heat (simmering water) melt unsweetened chocolate. When chocolate starts to melt, alternate adding in cocoa/sugar and milk slowly, while still heating, until smooth. Remove from heat.

3. Beat egg with remaining sugar until light and fluffy.

4. Slowly add egg mixture to melted chocolate. Return to heat and cook about three minutes over medium heat or until temperature reaches 160°F. Remove from heat and add cream and vanilla.

5. Cool mixture to 40°F in your refrigerator.

6. Just before placing mixture into ice cream freezer, mix peanut butter with 1 cup ice cream mixture and add back into mixture and mix until combined.

7. Transfer cold mixture to the ice cream freezer and follow manufacturer's guidelines.

# Chocolate Banana Ice Cream

3 oz. semisweet chocolate naps

2 cups whole milk

2 cups heavy cream

1 cup half-and-half

1½ cups table sugar

5 medium ripe bananas

1 TB. vanilla extract

**Yield:** About 2 quarts

**Prep time:** 20 minutes

**Cook time:** 10 minutes

1. In a blender place peeled bananas with sugar, and purée.

2. Over top of double boiler over low heat (simmering water) melt chocolate. When chocolate is melted, slowly add 1 cup whole milk, mixing until smooth. Remove from heat.

3. In a mixing bowl combine melted chocolate, remaining milk, cream, vanilla, and bananas. Mix well.

4. Cool mixture to 40°F in your refrigerator.

5. Transfer cold mixture to the ice cream freezer and follow manufacturer's guidelines.

# German Chocolate Ice Cream

4 egg yolks

5 oz. semisweet chocolate naps

1 cup whole milk

1½ cups sugar

3 cups light cream

2 cups whipping cream

1 TB. vanilla

**Yield:** About 2 quarts

**Prep time:** 40 minutes

**Cook time:** 15 minutes

1. Beat egg yolks and sugar until light and fluffy. Add in 1 cup whipping cream, and mix.

2. In a heavy saucepan over medium heat combine light cream and egg mixture. Cook to 160°F or until mixture coats back of spoon. Remove from heat.

3. Place mix in refrigerator until chocolate is ready.

4. In a double boiler over low heat (simmering water) melt chocolate. When melted, slowly add milk and mix until smooth. Remove from heat. Allow mixture to cool for two minutes.

5. Very slowly add warm chocolate to egg mixture and blend until smooth. Add light cream and whipping cream and mix until well blended.

6. Cool mixture to 40°F in your refrigerator.

7. Transfer cold mixture to the ice cream freezer and follow manufacturer's guidelines.

# Chocolate Cheesecake Ice Cream

2 (8-oz.) pkgs. cream cheese, softened

2 egg yolks

2 cups whole milk

1½ cups unsweetened cocoa powder

1½ cups table sugar

2 cups whipping cream

1 TB. vanilla extract

**Yield:** About 2 quarts

**Prep time:** 35 minutes

**Cook time:** 15 minutes

1. Mix sugar and unsweetened cocoa powder together as it will incorporate faster into the other ingredients.

2. Beat egg yolks, sugar, and cocoa mixture until fluffy. Add 1 cup milk and mix.

3. In a double boiler over medium heat place egg mixture. Cook until temperature reaches 160°F (coats back of spoon). Remove from heat.

4. In a mixing bowl, with an electric hand mixer, blend, alternating egg mixture, whipping cream, cream cheese, and sugar/cocoa mixture. Blend until smooth (no lumps).

5. Add cocoa mixture to mixing bowl and combine.

6. Cool mixture to 40°F in your refrigerator.

7. Transfer cold mixture to the ice cream freezer and follow manufacturer's guidelines.

# Chocolate Almond Ice Cream

5 oz. unsweetened chocolate

3 cups whole milk

1½ cups sugar

2 egg yolks

2 cups heavy cream

2 tsp. almond extract

1 tsp. vanilla extract

Optional: Chop ¾ cup almonds

**Yield:** About 2 quarts

**Prep time:** 35 minutes

**Cook time:** 20 minutes

1. Beat eggs with sugar until light and fluffy.

2. In a heavy saucepan over medium heat, cook egg mixture with two cup whole milk until temperature reaches 160°F (coats back of spoon). Remove from heat. Cover with plastic wrap and place in refrigerator until chocolate is ready.

3. In a double boiler over low heat (simmering water) melt unsweetened chocolate. When melted, slowly add 1 cup whole milk, mix until smooth. Remove from heat. Cool for two minutes.

4. Combine chocolate with egg mixture, heavy cream, vanilla and almond extract. Mix well.

5. Cool mixture to 40°F in your refrigerator.

6. Transfer cold mixture to the ice cream freezer and follow manufacturer's guidelines.

# Irish Chocolate Ice Cream

4 oz. brown bread (wheat)

10 TB. whiskey

1 cup table sugar

4 egg yolks

2 cups heavy cream

2 cups light cream

1 cup whole milk

3 oz. semisweet chocolate naps

| **Yield:** About 2 quarts |
| **Prep time:** 40 minutes |
| **Cook time:** 20 minutes |

1. Cut brown bread into small pieces and soak in the whiskey until liquid is absorbed.

2. Beat egg yolks and sugar until fluffy.

3. In a heavy saucepan over medium heat, stirring constantly, combine egg mixture and 2 cups light cream. Cook until temperature reaches 160°F (coats back of spoon). Remove from heat. Cover with plastic and refrigerate until chocolate is ready.

4. In a double boiler over low heat (simmering water) melt chocolate. When melted, slowly add whole milk, and blend until smooth. Remove from heat.

5. In a blender, place soaked bread 2 cups heavy cream. Blend until smooth.

6. In large bowl combine chocolate, egg mixture, and bread. Mix well.

7. Cool mixture to 40°F in your refrigerator.

8. Transfer cold mixture to the ice cream freezer and follow manufacturer's guidelines.

# Mocha Ice Cream

3 egg yolks

⅔ cup unsweetened cocoa
powder

3 TB. instant coffee

2 cups whipping cream

2 cups light cream

1 cup whole milk

1⅓ cups table sugar

1½ tsp. vanilla extract

| | |
|---|---|
| **Yield:** About 2 quarts | |
| **Prep time:** 25 minutes | |
| **Cook time:** 10 minutes | |

1. Beat egg yolks until light and fluffy.

2. In a heavy saucepan over medium heat cook eggs with 2 cups milk until temperature reaches 160°F (coats back of spoon). Remove from heat.

3. Mix cocoa, coffee, and sugar together and slowly add to hot egg mixture. Blend until added ingredients are dissolved. Add heavy cream, light cream and vanilla extract and mix well.

4. Cool mixture to 40°F in your refrigerator.

5. Transfer cold mixture to the ice cream freezer and follow manufacturer's guidelines.

# Chocolate Malted Ice Cream

2 oz. semisweet chocolate naps

2 oz. unsweetened chocolate naps

1 cup malt

1 cup table sugar

5 cups light cream

2 tsp. vanilla extract

**Yield:** About 2 quarts

**Prep time:** 20 minutes

**Cook time:** 10 minutes

1. In a double boiler melt chocolates over low heat. Remove from heat and slowly add 2 cups of light cream. Blend until mixture is smooth and creamy.

2. Mix malt and sugar together.

3. In a mixing bowl blend malt mixture with light cream, vanilla, and chocolate mixture. Mix until malt mixture is totally dissolved.

4. Cool mixture to 40°F in your refrigerator.

5. Transfer cold mixture to the ice cream freezer and follow manufacturer's guidelines.

# Chocolate Mint Ice Cream

3 oz. semisweet chocolate naps

2 egg yolks

1 cup table sugar

3 cups whipping cream

2 cups evaporated milk

2 tsp. peppermint extract (or to taste)

**Yield:** About 2 quarts

**Prep time:** 25 minutes

**Cook time:** 15 minutes

1. Beat egg yolks and sugar until light and fluffy.

2. In a heavy saucepan over medium heat cook egg mixture with 2 cups whipping cream until mixture reaches 160°F. Remove from heat. Cover in plastic wrap and place in refrigerator until chocolate is ready.

3. In a double boiler over low heat melt chocolate. When melted, slowly add 1 cup whipping cream. Mix until smooth and creamy. Remove from heat.

4. Blend egg mixture, chocolate mixture, evaporated milk, and peppermint extract.

5. Cool mixture to 40°F in your refrigerator.

6. Transfer cold mixture to the ice cream freezer and follow manufacturer's guidelines.

# Old-Fashioned Chocolate Ice Cream

¾ cup unsweetened cocoa powder

1¾ cups table sugar

1 TB. cornstarch

1 (12-oz.) can evaporated milk

2 cups heavy cream

1 cup half-and-half

2 TB. vanilla

**Yield:** About 2 quarts

**Prep time:** 30 minutes

**Cook time:** 18 minutes

1. Mix cocoa powder, sugar, and cornstarch together.

2. In a heavy saucepan combine cocoa, sugar, cornstarch, and evaporated milk. Cook over low heat until mixture starts to thicken. Heat to 160°F. Remove from heat and place in ice bath.

3. When mixture is cool, in a mixing bowl add the remaining ingredients. Blend well.

4. Cool mixture to 40°F in your refrigerator.

5. Transfer cold mixture to the ice cream freezer and follow manufacturer's guidelines.

# Chocolate Mud Ice Cream

1 (5.1-oz.) package chocolate
instant pudding

2 (14-oz.) cans sweetened
condensed milk

3½ cups light cream

1½ tsp. vanilla extract

1 cup chopped pecans

**Yield:** About 2 quarts

**Prep time:** 15 minutes

**Cook time:** None

1. In a large mixing bowl add instant pudding with light cream. Beat until well mixed and slightly thickened.

2. Add condensed milk and vanilla, and blend well.

3. Cool mixture to 40°F in your refrigerator.

4. Transfer cold mixture to the ice cream freezer and follow manufacturer's guidelines.

5. Just before ice cream is frozen, add pecans to ice cream freezer or wait until ice cream is out of the freezer and quickly add pecans.

# Fudge Buttermilk Ice Cream

⅔ cup unsweetened cocoa powder

1½ cups table sugar

1½ cups half-and-half

4 cups buttermilk

1 tsp. vanilla extract

**Yield:** About 2 quarts

**Prep time:** 30 minutes

**Cook time:** 15 minutes

1. Combine cocoa with sugar until combined.

2. In a heavy saucepan over medium heat, cook cocoa mixture with ½ cup half-and-half until sugar is dissolved. Remove from heat and cool.

3. Beat buttermilk and vanilla together until smooth.

4. Combine cocoa mixture with buttermilk mixture; mix well.

5. Cool mixture to 40°F in your refrigerator.

6. Transfer cold mixture to the ice cream freezer and follow manufacturer's guidelines.

# Rocky Road Ice Cream

⅓ cup unsweetened cocoa powder

1 cup table sugar

2 cups whole milk

1 oz. semisweet chocolate square

2 cups heavy cream

1 cup miniature marshmallows

1 tsp. vanilla extract

½ cup chopped almonds or pecans

| |
|---|
| **Yield:** About 2 quarts |
| **Prep time:** 30 minutes |
| **Cook time:** None |

1. Mix sugar and cocoa together.

2. Over medium heat in a heavy saucepan add 2 cups whole milk to sugar mixture. Heat until all the ingredients are dissolved. Remove from heat and place in ice bath to cool.

3. When mixture is cool, add in vanilla and heavy cream.

4. Coarsely chop or grate semi-sweet chocolate square.

5. Add grated or chopped chocolate, marshmallows, and nuts to the liquid mixture and mix.

6. Cool mixture to 40°F in your refrigerator.

7. Transfer cold mixture to the ice cream freezer and follow manufacturer's guidelines.

**Variations:**

For 2 quarts of ice cream you should use about 1 to 1½ cups of the ripple (swirl) sauce. Your ripple should always be at room temperature.

To add to chocolate ice cream, I suggest raspberry, strawberry, cranberry, and pineapple fruit purées for rippling.

Popular add-ins in ice cream today are multiple ripples, nuts, and candy pieces.

Add-ins such as chopped candy bars, piecrust, other baked goods, and candy pieces should be kept as cold as possible before adding to the ice cream.

# Chapter 6

# Fruit-Flavor Recipes

## In This Chapter

- ◎ Why freshness is important
- ◎ Creativity can be fun
- ◎ Helpful hints for using fruit

After vanilla and chocolate, the most popular ice cream flavors throughout the years have been fruits. One of the great things about fruits is that there are so many different kinds to choose from. Odds are, there are several fruit flavors that you like, even if you're a picky eater.

## The Advantage of Fresh Fruit

When large commercial plants make fruit-flavored ice cream products, they generally use extract flavorings and processed purées, simply because it would be impractical for them to use fresh fruit. However, in many small ice cream shops you can get ice cream made with fresh fruits—and you can definitely taste the difference.

You can also choose fruits that are indigenous to your region, or prepare ethnic preferences like coconut, papaya, or ginger.

> **The Real Scoop**
>
> Experimenting with the endless variety of fruit flavors at home is not only productive, but also so much more fun. While researching for this book I had several pleasant surprises with fun fruits such as cranberry (our local fruit here on Cape Cod) and fig ice cream, both with great results.

# Tips for Using Fruit

With most fruits, because they contain water, you can expect a little more iciness in your finished product. Using a gelatin stabilizer and a little heavier cream does help. In many of these recipes, the flavors are complimented by the use of frozen fruit concentrates along with the fresh puréed fruit. Also, with most fruit it is imperative that it is as ripe as possible before preparing as a flavor. You will also need to vary the use of sugar depending on your own special tastes. For example, cranberry, grapefruit, and several others seem to taste stronger and most natural when kept on the tart side, but others need a little more sugar to help bring out the flavor.

> **Avoid a Meltdown**
>
> If you are making fruit recipes, it's important to plan ahead. You will probably need to allow time for the fruit to ripen.

As with any fresh produce, make sure you use safe handling practices to clean and wash your fruit products; some fruits have been shown to be contaminated with high amounts of bacteria. (Note: there is a good guide at http://fruitandvegetablesafety.tamu.edu/Consumers/GeneralSafety.pdf

# The Most Popular Fruit Flavors

When it comes to ice cream, strawberry is the most popular fruit variety. Banana and orange are also leading fruit flavors.

# Be Creative

Strawberry may be most popular ice cream fruit flavor, but it's definitely not your only choice. One fun thing about using fruit flavors is the endless number of unique blends you can come up with. Combinations of two different fruits like banana and strawberry can make a good match. Using your imagination and common sense to experiment with a few such combos can be both fun and rewarding.

### Avoid a Meltdown

Surprisingly, most fresh fruits contain less sugar than ice cream mix. If you add a large volume of fruit, diluting out the overall sugar content, this will give you problems with your freezing point. Also, some fruits contain a substantial amount of acid (lemon, oranges) and some, such as fresh pineapple, contain enzymes that "digest" and potentially curdle the milk proteins. In either case, your ice cream may end up having a bit of a "cream cheese"-like texture to it. Nothing to be alarmed about—it's entirely safe—just a novel character when using some fruits.

Be sure to chop fruit into small pieces. Large chunks of fruit can prevent the dasher from working properly. I generally purée all fruits before using them in ice cream mixtures. I prefer, even in my ice cream shop, to have the total volume of the fruit all in a puree, to get the full taste of the fruit. But some like to keep small pieces of soft fruit in the finished ice cream to provide a nice visual cue of the added fruit. Like any added product, you should cool the fruit to at least refrigeration temperature (40°F) before adding to the ice cream freezer. This will allow the ice cream to freeze fast and prevent some iciness.

### The Real Scoop

Recipes with fruit and sugar are best when blended together and chilled overnight.

# Blueberry Ice Cream

2 TB. gelatin

½ cup warm water

1½ pints clean blueberries

2 cups whole milk

1 cup sugar

2 cups whipping cream

| Yield: About 2 quarts |
| :---: |
| Prep time: 45 minutes |
| Cook time: None |

1. Dissolve gelatin in warm water until completely dehydrated (10 to 15 minutes).

2. Purée blueberries in a blender. Strain blueberries, save pulp, and return to blender; add dissolved gelatin, whole milk, and sugar. Blend until smooth (at this time you can add back in a little of the pulp for more flavor).

3. In a mixing bowl combine whipping cream and blueberry purée mixture and mix well.

4. Cool mixture to 40°F in your refrigerator.

5. Transfer cold mixture to the ice cream freezer and follow manufacturer's guidelines.

 **Cool Tips**

If berries are not sweet enough, you may add more sugar.

# Kiwi Ice Cream

1 pint kiwi purée (9 to 10 kiwis)
1¼ cups table sugar
4 cups light cream
2 drops green food color

**Yield:** About 2 quarts

**Prep time:** 25 minutes

**Cook time:** 10 minutes

1. Peel and purée kiwis in blender.

2. In a heavy saucepan over low heat mix light cream with sugar until sugar is dissolved.

3. Remove from heat and place in refrigerator until cool.

4. When cool, add light cream and food coloring.

5. Cool mixture to 40°F in your refrigerator.

6. Transfer cold mixture to the ice cream freezer and follow manufacturer's guidelines.

### Cool Tips

You may have to add more sugar to your taste.

# Strawberry Banana Ice Cream

1¼ cups strawberry purée (1 pint strawberries)
¼ cup sugar
1 cup banana purée (3 large)
2 cups half-and-half
2 cups whipping cream

**Yield:** About 2 quarts

**Prep time:** 35 minutes

**Cook time:** None

1. Purée clean strawberries with sugar and peeled bananas in a blender.

2. In a large mixing bowl combine purées, half-and-half, and whipping cream.

3. Cool mixture to 40°F in your refrigerator.

4. Transfer cold mixture to the ice cream freezer and follow manufacturer's guidelines.

# Apricot Ice Cream

1½ pints apricot purée
(8 or 9 apricots)

¾ cup table sugar

2 cups heavy cream

2 cups light cream

| **Yield:** About 2 quarts |
|---|
| **Prep time:** 25 minutes |
| **Cook time:** None |

1. Wash apricots and dry (do not peel).

2. Purée apricots with sugar in a blender.

3. In a mixing bowl add heavy cream and light cream to purée and mix until blended.

4. Cool mixture to 40°F in your refrigerator.

5. Transfer cold mixture to the ice cream freezer and follow manufacturer's guidelines.

# Banana Ice Cream

8 large bananas

1 cup table sugar

3 cups light cream

2 cups half-and-half

| **Yield:** About 2 quarts |
|---|
| **Prep time:** 15 minutes |
| **Cook time:** None |

1. Peel and purée bananas in a blender with sugar.

2. In mixing bowl add creams and purée, and mix until well blended.

3. Cool mixture to 40°F in your refrigerator.

4. Transfer cold mixture to the ice cream freezer and follow manufacturer's guidelines.

# Rhubarb Ice Cream

8 long stalks of rhubarb
(1 pint purée)

1½ cups water

½ cup rhubarb syrup

¾ cup table sugar

2 cups heavy cream

2 cups light cream

**Yield:** About 2 quarts

**Prep time:** 45 minutes

**Cook time:** 25 minutes

1. Remove all leaves and ends from stalks, cut into small pieces, and steam over 1½ cups of water until soft.

2. Remove rhubarb to blender and purée. (Save steam water.)

3. In a saucepan over high heat add sugar to steam water and reduce by half.

4. Remove from heat.

5. When mixture has cooled, add heavy cream, light cream, and purée, and stir until well blended.

6. Cool mixture to 40°F in your refrigerator.

7. Transfer cold mixture to the ice cream freezer and follow manufacturer's guidelines.

# Mango Ice Cream

6 large, ripe mangos

¼ cup table sugar

2 cups heavy cream

2 cups light cream

**Yield:** About 2 quarts

**Prep time:** 40 minutes

**Cook time:** None

1. Peel ripe mangos and purée with sugar in blender. (You may need to add some cream.)

2. In a mixing bowl add purée to heavy cream and light cream; blend until incorporated.

3. Cool mixture to 40°F in your refrigerator.

4. Transfer cold mixture to the ice cream freezer and follow manufacturer's guidelines.

# Cantaloupe Ice Cream

1 large, very ripe cantaloupe
(1 to 1½ pints purée)

½ cup table sugar

2 egg yolks

1 cup whole milk

3 cups whipping cream

**Yield:** About 2 quarts

**Prep time:** 40 minutes

**Cook time:** 15 minutes

1. Peel cantaloupe and purée in blender.

2. Beat egg yolks and sugar until light and fluffy.

3. In a double boiler over medium heat combine egg mixture and milk, cook until mixture reaches 160°F (coats back of spoon).

4. Remove from heat, cover with plastic wrap, and cool in refrigerator.

5. When cool, add cantaloupe and whipping cream to egg mixture and mix well.

6. Cool mixture to 40°F in your refrigerator.

7. Transfer cold mixture to the ice cream freezer and follow manufacturer's guidelines.

# Ginger Ice Cream

1 cup ginger, peeled and chopped

1½ cups water

1 cup table sugar

5 egg yolks

2 cups whole milk

2 cups heavy cream

| |
| --- |
| **Yield:** About 2 quarts |
| **Prep time:** 60 minutes |
| **Cook time:** 25 minutes |

1. Place peeled and chopped ginger in heavy saucepan with water to cover; cook until soft.

2. Remove ginger from water and purée in blender with 1 cup of milk (save ginger water).

3. In a heavy saucepan over high heat boil ginger water and sugar down to a syrup consistency, about 4 minutes (¼ to ½ cup).

4. Beat egg yolks until light and foamy.

5. In a heavy saucepan over medium heat cook eggs with whole milk and ginger purée to 160°F (coats back of spoon).

6. Remove from heat, mix in the ginger syrup, and place in ice bath to cool.

7. When cool, add heavy cream and cool mixture to 40°F in your refrigerator.

8. Transfer cold mixture to the ice cream freezer and follow manufacturer's guidelines.

# Avocado Ice Cream

1 pkg. frozen avocados
(1½ pints purée)

1 cup table sugar

2 cups whole milk

2 cups whipping cream

**Yield:** About 2 quarts

**Prep time:** 30 minutes

**Cook time:** 10 minutes

1. Thaw avocados and purée in blender with whipping cream.

2. In a saucepan heat milk with sugar until sugar is dissolved.

3. Remove from heat. Refrigerate until cool.

4. In a mixing bowl combine cooled milk mixture with avocado purée and mix well.

5. Cool mixture to 40°F in your refrigerator.

6. Transfer cold mixture to the ice cream freezer and follow manufacturer's guidelines.

# Grapefruit Ice Cream

2 TB. gelatin (2 oz.)

½ cup warm water

1 (15-oz.) can grapefruit sections in juice

1 (12-oz.) can grapefruit frozen concentrate

2 cups half-and-half

2 cups whipping cream

| | |
|---|---|
| **Yield:** About 2 quarts | |
| **Prep time:** 30 minutes | |
| **Cook time:** None | |

1. Place gelatin in warm water and let sit until completely dehydrated (10 to 15 minutes).

2. In a blender grind grapefruit section without juice.

3. Add grapefruit concentrate and gelatin to the blender and mix.

4. In a mixing bowl add half-and-half and whipping cream to grapefruit mixture and stir until well blended.

5. Cool mixture to 40°F in your refrigerator.

6. Transfer cold mixture to the ice cream freezer and follow manufacturer's guidelines.

# Cherry Ice Cream

2 TB. gelatin (2 oz.)

½ cup warm water

3 lbs. cherries, clean and pitted

2 cups whipping cream

2 cups heavy cream

**Yield:** About 2 quarts

**Prep time:** 40 minutes

**Cook time:** None

1. Place gelatin in warm water and let sit until completely dehydrated (10 to 15 minutes).

2. In a blender grind clean pitted cherries (you may have to add a little cream).

3. Add gelatin to ground cherries in the blender, and continue to grind for 30 seconds.

4. Place ground cherries and gelatin in a mixing bowl along with the whipping cream and heavy cream. Mix well.

5. Cool mixture to 40°F in your refrigerator.

6. Transfer cold mixture to the ice cream freezer and follow manufacturer's guidelines.

# Grape Ice Cream

2 TB. gelatin (2 oz.)

½ cup warm water

2 (12-oz.) cans grape concentrate (thawed)

1 cup whole grapes

2 cups heavy cream

2 cups light cream

| **Yield:** About 2 quarts |
| --- |
| **Prep time:** 30 minutes |
| **Cook time:** None |

1. Place gelatin in warm water and allow to sit until completely dehydrated (10 to 15 minutes).

2. In a blender grind grapes with gelatin mixture.

3. In a large mixing bowl mix concentrate with heavy cream and light cream. Add in ground grape mixture.

4. Cool mixture to 40°F in your refrigerator.

5. Transfer cold mixture to the ice cream freezer and follow manufacturer's guidelines.

# Apple Ice Cream

2 TB. gelatin (2 oz.)

½ cup warm water

2 (12-oz.) cans frozen apple concentrate (thawed)

1 cup apple sauce (no sugar added)

2 cups whipping cream

2 cups light cream

| **Yield:** About 2 quarts |
| --- |
| **Prep time:** 30 minutes |
| **Cook time:** None |

1. Place gelatin in warm water and allow to sit until completely dehydrated (10 to 15 minutes).

2. In a blender combine apple sauce and gelatin mixture.

3. Combine apple sauce and gelatin mixture with whipping cream and light cream in a large mixing bow. Mix until well incorporated.

4. Cool mixture to 40°F in your refrigerator.

5. Transfer cold mixture to the ice cream freezer and follow manufacturer's guidelines.

# Date Ice Cream

1½ pints date purée (24–26 large pitted dates)

2 cups milk

2 cups heavy cream

| **Yield:** About 2 quarts |
| --- |
| **Prep time:** 35 minutes |
| **Cook time:** None |

1. In a blender grind pitted dates until smooth. Add milk as needed.

2. Combine remaining milk and heavy cream in a mixing bowl with purée. Mix well.

3. Cool mixture to 40°F in your refrigerator.

4. Transfer cold mixture to the ice cream freezer and follow manufacturer's guidelines.

# Orange Ice Cream

2 TB. gelatin (2 oz.)

½ cup warm water

2 (12-oz.) cans orange frozen concentrate (thawed)

2 sweet oranges

1 cup milk

2 cups light cream

1 cup whipping cream

**Yield:** About 2 quarts

**Prep time:** 30 minutes

**Cook time:** None

1. Dissolve gelatin in warm water and allow to sit until completely dehydrated (10 to 15 minutes).

2. Roll oranges on a counter to facilitate juicing.

3. Cut and juice oranges to get ¾ cup. Remove pulp from 1 orange. Grind pulp, juice, and gelatin in blender.

4. In mixing bowl combine orange concentrate, juice mixture, milk, light cream, and whipping cream. Blend well.

5. Cool mixture to 40°F in your refrigerator.

6. Transfer cold mixture to the ice cream freezer and follow manufacturer's guidelines.

# Fig Ice Cream

12 oz. dried figs

2 cup water

¾ cup table sugar

3 cups milk

1½ cups whipping cream

**Yield:** About 2 quarts

**Prep time:** 45 minutes

**Cook time:** 20 minutes

1. Place figs and water in a heavy sauce pan and cook until very soft. Drain figs and save one cup of the cooking water.

2. Place soft figs in a blender. Add sugar and saved cooking water. Blend until smooth. You may have to add a little milk.

3. In a mixing bowl add fig mixture, remaining milk, and whipping cream, and mix until smooth.

4. Cool mixture to 40°F in your refrigerator.

5. Transfer cold mixture to the ice cream freezer and follow manufacturer's guidelines.

# Cranberry Ice Cream

2 TB. cornstarch

1 (12-oz.) can cranberry concentrate (thawed)

¼ cup table sugar

1 (6-oz.) pkg. dried cranberries

2 cups half-and-half

2 cups whipping cream

1 cup milk

**Yield:** About 2 quarts

**Prep time:** 35 minutes

**Cook time:** 15 minutes

1. In the top of a double boiler over medium heat combine cornstarch, sugar, and milk. Cook until thick and mixture reaches 160°F.

2. Remove from heat and place in an ice bath until cool.

3. In a blender grind dried cranberries with half-and-half.

4. Combine cooled cornstarch mixture, ground cranberries, whipping cream, and cranberry concentrate. Blend thoroughly.

5. Cool mixture to 40°F in your refrigerator.

6. Transfer cold mixture to the ice cream freezer and follow manufacturer's guidelines.

# Coconut Ice Cream

1 (15-oz.) can cream of coconut

½ cup coconut flakes

1 cup milk

2 cups heavy cream

2 cups light cream

**Yield:** About 2 quarts

**Prep time:** 30 minutes

**Cook time:** None

1. Combine milk and coconut flakes. Soak 10 minutes.

2. In a mixing bowl combine and mix soaked flakes with cream of coconut, heavy cream, and light cream.

3. Cool mixture to 40°F in your refrigerator.

4. Transfer cold mixture to the ice cream freezer and follow manufacturer's guidelines.

# Pineapple Ice Cream

2 TB. gelatin (2 oz.)

½ cup warm water

2 (12-oz.) cans pineapple concentrate (thawed)

1 cup crushed pineapple without juice

2 cups whipping cream

1 cup light cream

| **Yield:** About 2 quarts |
| **Prep time:** 30 minutes |
| **Cook time:** None |

1. Place gelatin in warm water and allow to sit until completely dehydrated (10 to 15 minutes).

2. Grind crushed pineapple and gelatin in a blender.

3. In a mixing bowl combine pineapple mixture with whipping cream, light cream, and pineapple concentrate and blend well.

4. Cool mixture to 40°F in your refrigerator.

5. Transfer cold mixture to the ice cream freezer and follow manufacturer's guidelines.

# Fresh Peach Ice Cream

2 TB. gelatin (2 oz.)

½ cup warm water

12 large, sweet peaches or enough to make 2 pints

1½ cups table sugar

1 cup whole milk

2 cups heavy cream

| |
|---|
| **Yield:** About 2 quarts |
| **Prep time:** 45 minutes |
| **Cook time:** None |

1. Place gelatin in warm water and allow to sit until completely dehydrated (10 to 15 minutes).

2. Wash, pit, and cut up peaches (do not peel).

3. In a blender purée peaches, sugar, gelatin, and milk until smooth.

4. Combine puréed mixture with heavy cream and mix well.

5. Cool mixture to 40°F in your refrigerator.

6. Transfer cold mixture to the ice cream freezer and follow manufacturer's guidelines.

# Fresh Strawberry Ice Cream

2 TB. cornstarch

1 cup whole milk

2 pints strawberries (puréed)

¾ cup table sugar

2 cups whipping cream

2–3 drops red food coloring

**Yield:** About 2 quarts

**Prep time:** 30 minutes

**Cook time:** 15 minutes

1. In a double boiler over medium heat combine cornstarch and whole milk. Cook until temperature reaches 160°F (coats back of spoon).

2. Remove from heat and place in an ice bath.

3. Clean and hull strawberries. Purée in blender with sugar.

4. Combine cornstarch mixture and puréed strawberries and whipping cream. Blend thoroughly.

5. Add food coloring if desired.

6. Cool mixture to 40°F in your refrigerator.

7. Transfer cold mixture to the ice cream freezer and follow manufacturer's guidelines.

### The Real Scoop

Fresh strawberry ice cream without food coloring is an off-white.

# Pumpkin Ice Cream

1 (15-oz.) can pumpkin

1 tsp. cinnamon

¾ tsp. Ginger

¾ tsp. Nutmeg

¾ cup table sugar

3 cups half-and-half

2 cups heavy cream

**Yield:** About 2 quarts

**Prep time:** 25 minutes

**Cook time:** None

1. Place all ingredients in mixing bowl and mix until well blended.

2. Cool mixture to 40°F in your refrigerator.

3. Transfer cold mixture to the ice cream freezer and follow manufacturer's guidelines.

# Lemon Ice Cream

4 egg yolks

2½ cups whole milk

3 large lemons

1 cup table sugar

¾ cup lemon juice

3 tsp. lemon zest

2 cups whipping cream

2 cups half-and-half

**Yield:** About 2 quarts

**Prep time:** 60 minutes

**Cook time:** 25 minutes

1. Zest 1 lemon and juice to ¾ cup.

2. Beat egg yolks with sugar until light and fluffy.

3. In the top of a double boiler over medium heat combine eggs, milk, sugar, and lemon zest.

4. Cook until temperature reaches 160°F (coats back of spoon).

5. Remove from heat and place in an ice bath.

6. When cool, add lemon juice, whipping cream and half-and-half and blend well.

7. Cool mixture to 40°F in your refrigerator.

8. Transfer cold mixture to the ice cream freezer and follow manufacturer's guidelines.

# Raspberry Ice Cream

2 TB. gelatin (2 oz.)

½ cup warm water

2 pints raspberries puréed to make 3 pints fresh or 3 (12-oz.) bags frozen

1 cup table sugar

1 cup whole milk

2 cups light cream

| **Yield:** About 2 quarts |
| **Prep time:** 30 minutes |
| **Cook time:** None |

1. Combine gelatin with water; let sit until completely dehydrated (10 to 15 minutes).

2. In a blender purée raspberries.

3. Strain raspberries (this step is optional).

4. Return raspberry purée to blender and add sugar, milk, and gelatin. Blend until smooth.

5. In a mixing bowl add light cream to puréed mixture and mix.

6. Cool mixture to 40°F in your refrigerator.

7. Transfer cold mixture to the ice cream freezer and follow manufacturer's guidelines.

# Prune Ice Cream

2 TB. gelatin (2 oz.)

½ cup warm water

20 oz. dried pitted prunes

3 cups whole milk

¼ cup table sugar

2 cups whipping cream

| | |
|---|---|
| **Yield:** About 2 quarts | |
| **Prep time:** 30 minutes | |
| **Cook time:** None | |

1. Dissolve gelatin in water and allow to sit until completely dehydrated (10 to 15 minutes).

2. In a blender purée prunes with milk and sugar.

3. Add gelatin to puréed prunes and blend until incorporated.

4. Combine purée with whipping cream.

5. Cool mixture to 40°F in your refrigerator.

6. Transfer cold mixture to the ice cream freezer and follow manufacturer's guidelines.

# Chapter 7

# Other Regular Flavor Recipes

## In This Chapter

- ☺ Different areas like different flavors
- ☺ How flavor popularity is determined
- ☺ Old favorites and new twists

For other regular flavors, I have included, not in any special order, many of the top-selling, possibly standard choices through the years. What seems to be a regular flavor in one area can be drastically different a few miles away. For example, I have a close friend who has an ice cream shop in Canada. In cones at his shop, Bubble Gum ice cream is one of the top three sellers, but in nearby Buffalo, New York, where he consults with several shops, the same flavor is not even in the top fifteen. The opposite is true with Cotton Candy ice cream; it is number three in Buffalo and number twenty in Canada. It is interesting to note that in general, cake-batter-flavored ice cream has defeated Oreo Cookie, but Cookie Dough still holds its own.

Research figures on what flavors are most regular or popular are gleaned from national supermarket sales figures and sales of major ice cream manufacturers. Annually those figures list vanilla in the 30 percent range and chocolate in the 9 to 10 percent bracket. The next level of public choice finds butter pecan, (or other special nut flavors) strawberry, chocolate chip, cookies in cream, vanilla fudge, and black raspberry in that order, each at 3 to 6 percent of the market. Mint chip, coffee, cherry, and caramel round out the popularity list at 1 to 2 percent of total sales.

Most of my flavors in this book have several variations, including mix-ins of nuts and candies, ripples (stripes), and possibly injecting all three. The choice of names could be "Chocolate Raspberry Banana Crunch Pie Ice Cream" or a title like "Banana Chocolate Pie Supreme" and so on. I have included many of the varieties, but once again just let your imagination run wild with combinations of your favorite mix-ins.

If you are a traditionalist, as I am, you can find included here many old-time flavors such as "Caramel" and "Coffee." I often feel that too many different ripples, candy chunks, and nuts tend to cover up or mask a delicious basic flavor, which should be enjoyed on its own merits.

### The Real Scoop

You might assume the folks in the warmer climates eat the most ice cream; not necessarily so. Per person, New Englanders are among the largest consumers of ice cream in the United States. In 1999, the citizens of Omaha, Nebraska, ate the most ice cream in that year.

# Caramel Ice Cream

2 cups table sugar

⅔ cup half-and-half

4 egg yolks

4 cups light cream

2 tsp. vanilla extract

**Yield:** About 2 quarts

**Prep time:** 60 minutes

**Cook time:** 40 minutes

1. In a heavy saucepan over medium-high heat, cook 1 cup sugar, stirring constantly until sugar becomes a deep golden brown, smooth syrup.

2. Heat ⅔ cup half-and-half in the microwave until hot. (Do not boil.) Add 1 cup sugar to the half-and-half and mix until sugar is dissolved.

3. Beat egg yolks until light and fluffy. Add half-and-half mixture and mix. Add light cream and mix well.

4. In the top of a double boiler over medium heat, cook egg mixture until mixture reaches 160°F. The USDA recommends (and so do we) that you cook this mixture to 160°F, using a reliable thermometer. Remove from heat and slowly add browned syrup mixture and vanilla. (If browned sugar has hardened, re-melt over low heat.) Remove from heat. Pour mixture into mixing bowl.

5. Cool mixture to 40°F in your refrigerator.

6. Place cold mixture into the ice cream freezer and freeze according to manufacturer's directions.

**Variations:**

1½ cups pecans, walnuts, macadamia, or almonds, chopped

1½ cups chocolate-covered cranberry or raisins

1½ cups any type candy, chopped

# Pistachio Ice Cream

1½ cups pistachio nuts (shelled and unsalted)

1 (3.4-oz.) pkg. instant pistachio pudding mix

2 cups whole milk

3 cups half-and-half

2 cups heavy cream

1 TB. vanilla extract

| | |
|---|---|
| **Yield:** About 2 quarts | |
| **Prep time:** 30 minutes | |
| **Cook time:** None | |

1. Grind pistachio nuts with milk in a blender until nuts are just flakes.

2. Add half-and-half and pistachio pudding mix to blender. Blend until incorporated.

3. Pour into a mixing bowl and add remaining heavy cream and vanilla.

4. Cool mixture to 40°F in your refrigerator.

5. Place cold mixture into the ice cream freezer and freeze according to manufacturer's directions.

**Variations:**

1 small can crushed pineapple, blended

1½ cups pistachios, walnuts, almonds, etc., chopped

### The Real Scoop

Certain regular flavors are so key to some people that an astrology-type prognosticator came up with a flavorology research compatibility chart for ice cream lovers. Here are two examples: If your favorite flavor is vanilla ice cream you are genuinely sincere, conservative, and get along well with strawberry ice cream lovers. If chocolate ice cream is your choice, you have a warm heart, take some chances, and are compatible with chocolate chip ice cream lovers.

# Cinnamon Ice Cream

4 egg yolks

2 cups whole milk

3 cups heavy cream

2 cups light cream

5 small cinnamon sticks

1 cup table sugar

1 TB. ground cinnamon

**Yield:** About 2 quarts

**Prep time:** 30 minutes

**Cook time:** 10 minutes

1. Beat egg yolks, cinnamon, and sugar until light and fluffy.

2. In the top of a double boiler over medium heat, add egg mixture, milk, and cinnamon sticks. Cook to 160°F (coats back of spoon). Remove from heat. Remove cinnamon sticks, place plastic wrap over mixture, place in refrigerator to cool.

3. When cool, combine egg mixture with heavy cream and light cream. Mix well.

4. Cool mixture to 40°F in your refrigerator.

5. Place cold mixture in the ice cream freezer and freeze according to manufacturer's directions.

**Variations:**

1½ cups graham cracker pieces

1½ cups walnuts, pecans, etc., chopped

# Grape Nuts Ice Cream

2 TB. unflavored gelatin (2 oz.)

½ cup warm water

1 cup table sugar

4 cups whipping cream

3 cups half-and-half

1 TB. vanilla extract

1 cup Grape Nuts cereal

**Yield:** About 2 quarts

**Prep time:** 25 minutes

**Cook time:** None

1. Place gelatin in warm water and let sit until completely dehydrated (10 to 15 minutes).

2. Combine sugar, whipping cream, half-and-half, vanilla extract, gelatin, and cereal in a large mixing bowl and mix until sugar and gelatin have been dissolved.

3. Cool mixture to 40°F in your refrigerator.

4. Place cold mixture in the ice cream freezer and freeze according to manufacturer's directions.

**Variation:**

1½ cups raisins

# Crème Brûlée Ice Cream

2½ cups table sugar

4 TB. water

6 egg yolks

3 cups heavy cream

3 cups half-and-half

2 tsp. vanilla extract

| **Yield:** About 2 quarts |
| **Prep time:** 30 minutes |
| **Cook time:** 15 minutes |

1. In a heavy saucepan combine sugar and water. Over medium heat, cook sugar mixture until sugar turns golden brown. Remove from heat.

2. Beat egg yolks until light and fluffy. Add half-and-half and place in the top of a double boiler over medium heat. Cook until temperature reaches 160°F. Remove from heat and slowly stir in sugar mixture. (If mixture has hardened, place on stove and re-melt over low heat.)

3. Place mixture in ice bath and allow to cool to room temperature.

4. In a large mixing bowl add cooled mixture, heavy cream, and vanilla. Mix well.

5. Cool mixture to 40°F in your refrigerator.

6. Place cold mixture into the ice cream freezer and follow manufacturer's directions.

# Peppermint Ice Cream

3 TB. cornstarch

2 cups whole milk

3 cups half-and-half

2 cups whipping cream

1¼ cups peppermint candies

1 TB. vanilla extract

5 TB. peppermint extract

| **Yield:** About 2 quarts |
| **Prep time:** 35 minutes |
| **Cook time:** 15 minutes |

1. Place cornstarch and milk in the top of a double boiler and cook over medium heat until cornstarch thickens. Remove from heat and cool.

2. Unwrap peppermint candies and place in a refrigerator freezer.

3. Combine cooled cornstarch with half-and-half, whipping cream, vanilla, and peppermint extract.

4. Remove candies from freezer and break into tiny pieces. Add to mixture and mix well.

5. Cool mixture to 40°F in your refrigerator.

6. Place cold mixture into the ice cream freezer and freeze according to manufacturer's directions.

**Variations:**

1½ mint candies, crushed

1½ cups chocolate chips

# Black Licorice Ice Cream

2 cups black licorice cut into small pieces

2 cups whole milk

4 egg yokes

1 cup table sugar

2 cups heavy cream

**Yield:** About 2 quarts

**Prep time:** 40 minutes

**Cook time:** 20 minutes

1. In a blender or food processor place the cut licorice and milk, and chop until it looks like small pieces of rice.

2. Beat eggs until creamy; add sugar and combine.

3. In a double boiler or heavy saucepan heat 1 cup whole milk and 1 cup half-and-half until hot. (DO NOT BOIL.)

4. Remove from heat and very slowly pour a little at a time into the egg/sugar mixture. Continue to add slowly until all the liquid is incorporated.

5. Return egg/sugar/milk mixture to the top of the double boiler and heat until mixture reaches 160°F or until it coats the back of a spoon.

6. Remove from heat and cool in an ice bath.

7. When mixture is cold to the touch add the licorice and heavy cream and mix well.

8. Cool to 40°F.

9. Follow manufacturer's directions for making ice cream.

# Maple Ice Cream

3 egg yolks

1 cup whole milk

2 cups pure maple syrup

2 cups heavy cream

2 cups light cream

| **Yield:** About 2 quarts |
|---|
| **Prep time:** 30 minutes |
| **Cook time:** 15 minutes |

1. Beat egg yolks until light and fluffy.

2. In the top of a double boiler over medium heat, cook eggs and whole milk until mixture reaches 160°F. Remove from heat and place in an ice bath.

3. Combine maple syrup, heavy cream, light cream, and cooled egg mixture. Stir until mixture is well blended.

4. Cool mixture to 40°F in your refrigerator.

5. Place cold mixture into the ice cream freezer and freeze according to manufacturer's directions.

**Variation:**

1½ cups walnuts, chopped

# Peanut Butter Ice Cream

2 TB. unflavored gelatin (2 oz.)

½ cup warm water

1¼ cups peanut butter (smooth or chunky)

1 cup table sugar

3 cups whole milk

3 cups whipping cream

1 TB. vanilla extract

**Yield:** About 2 quarts

**Prep time:** 30 minutes

**Cook time:** None

1. Dissolve gelatin in warm water until completely dehydrated (10 to 15 minutes).

2. Place sugar, milk, and dissolved gelatin in a blender. Blend until gelatin is incorporated. Add peanut butter and continue to blend until mixture is smooth. (You may have to add more cream to mixture.)

3. Combine peanut butter mixture with whipping cream and vanilla extract and mix well.

4. Cool mixture to 40°F in your refrigerator.

5. Place cold mixture into the ice cream freezer and freeze according to manufacturer's directions.

**Variations:**

1½ cups nuts, chopped

1½ cup chocolate or butterscotch bits

1½ cups candies or chocolate bars, crushed

Ripples: jelly, maple syrup, chocolate, caramel, etc.

# Coffee Ice Cream

3 TB. instant coffee

1½ cups table sugar

7 cups light cream

2 tsp. vanilla extract

**Yield:** About 2 quarts

**Prep time:** 25 minutes

**Cook time:** 10 minutes

1. In a heavy saucepan over low heat dissolve instant coffee and sugar in 3 cups light cream. (Do not boil.) When mixture is dissolved, remove from heat and let cool in refrigerator.

2. Add vanilla extract and remaining light cream to coffee mixture and mix well.

3. Cool mixture to 40°F in your refrigerator.

4. Place cold mixture into the ice cream freezer and freeze according to manufacturer's directions.

**Variations:**

1½ cups nuts, chopped

½ cup whiskey

Ripples: chocolate, caramel, butterscotch, or praline

# Honey Ice Cream

3 TB. cornstarch

1 cup whole milk

1½ cups pure light honey

3 cups heavy cream

3 cups half-and-half

| Yield: About 2 quarts |
| --- |
| **Prep time:** 30 minutes |
| **Cook time:** 15 minutes |

1. Place cornstarch and milk in the top of a double boiler and cook over medium heat until mixture forms a smooth paste. Cool in the refrigerator.

2. Add cooled cornstarch to honey, heavy cream and half-and-half and mix well

3. Cool mixture to 40°F in your refrigerator.

4. Place cold mixture into the ice cream freezer and freeze according to manufacturer's directions.

**Variations:**

1½ cups walnuts, pecans, almonds, etc.

1½ cups granola and other crunch cereals

1½ graham cracker pieces

1½ raisins

1½ cups dates, chopped

# Brown Sugar-Pecan Ice Cream

3 egg yolks

2 cups whole milk

2 cups light brown sugar

2 TB. butter

2 cups whipping cream

2 cups light cream

1 TB. vanilla extract

1 cup chopped pecans

**Yield:** About 2 quarts

**Prep time:** 40 minutes

**Cook time:** 15 minutes

1. Beat egg yolks until light and fluffy.

2. In the top of a double boiler over medium heat, combine egg yolks with 1 cup milk, and cook until mixture reaches 160°F (coats back of spoon). When cooked, remove from heat and place in an ice bath.

3. In a heavy saucepan melt butter and brown sugar. Continue to cook over medium heat for 1 minute. Brown sugar will darken. Remove from heat and slowly pour in remaining milk. If needed, return mixture to heat to incorporate milk, but do not boil. Cool until mixture is just barely warm.

4. In a mixing bowl combine egg mixture with brown sugar mixture, whipping cream, light cream and vanilla extract. Mix well.

5. Cool mixture to 40°F in your refrigerator.

6. Place cold mixture into the ice cream freezer and freeze according to manufacturer's directions.

7. Just before ice cream is ready to be removed from ice cream freezer, add chopped pecans. Pecans can also be added while ice cream is being removed from freezer; just add to mixture and stir.

# Butterscotch Ice Cream

3 TB. cornstarch

2 cups whole milk

3 TB. butter

1½ cups light brown sugar

½ cup dark corn syrup

2 cups light cream

2 cups half-and-half

1 tsp. vanilla

| **Yield:** About 2 quarts |
| --- |
| **Prep time:** 40 minutes |
| **Cook time:** 20 minutes |

1. Cook cornstarch and milk in a heavy saucepan over medium heat, until mixture becomes a smooth paste. Remove from heat and cool in refrigerator.

2. In a heavy saucepan over medium heat, melt butter and add brown sugar. Cook until brown sugar is melted and darkened. (Do not burn.) Remove from heat and let cool.

3. When both mixtures have cooled to room temperature, place them in a large mixing bowl and add corn syrup, whipping cream, light cream, and vanilla. Mix until well incorporated.

4. Cool mixture to 40°F in your refrigerator.

5. Place cold mixture into the ice cream freezer and freeze according to manufacturer's directions.

**Variations:**

1½ cups cookie dough pieces, very cold

1½ cups nuts, chopped

1½ cups peanut brittle, chopped

1½ cups chocolate or butterscotch bits

1½ cups candy bars, crushed

# Hazelnut Ice Cream

4 egg yolks

1¼ cups table sugar

6 cups light cream

1½ cups hazelnuts skinned

3 TB. hazelnut syrup

3 TB. Frangelico liqueur

**Yield:** About 2 quarts

**Prep time:** 40 minutes

**Cook time:** 20 minutes

1. Preheat oven to 350°F. Place hazelnuts on a cookie sheet and bake for 15 minutes. Remove from heat and cool for 15 minutes. Wrap nuts in a thick kitchen towel and rub to loosen and remove the skins. Let cool completely.

2. Grind the nuts finely in a blender or food processor.

3. Beat egg yolks and sugar together until light and fluffy.

4. In the top of a double boiler, over medium heat, combine egg mixture with 2 cups light cream. Cook until temperature reached 160°F (coats back of spoon). (Do not boil.) Remove from heat and place in an ice bath.

5. When cool, remove from ice bath. In a large mixing bowl add remaining light cream, Frangelico, hazelnut syrup, and the ground hazelnuts. Mix thoroughly.

6. Cool mixture to 40°F in your refrigerator.

7. Place cooled mixture into the ice cream freezer and freeze according to manufacturer's directions.

# Amaretto Ice Cream

¾ cup amaretto syrup (directions below)

6 egg yolks

2 cups whole milk

2 cups half-and-half

3 cups whipping cream

½ cup amaretto liqueur

**Yield:** About 2 quarts

**Prep time:** 45 minutes

**Cook time:** 30 minutes

For amaretto syrup:

1. Place 1½ cups of amaretto liqueur in a heavy saucepan.

2. Over high heat reduce liquid to ¾ cup. Let cool.

3. When cool it may be very thick and may have to be placed in the microwave to melt for about 15 seconds.

For ice cream:

1. In a mixing bowl beat the eggs until light and fluffy.

2. In the top of a double boiler, combine milk and eggs. Cook until mixture reaches 160°F (coats back of spoon).

3. In a large mixing bowl add half-and-half, whipping cream, and ½ cup amaretto liqueur. Mix well.

4. Add egg mixture to cream mixture in the mixing bowl and mix thoroughly.

5. Cool mixture to 40°F in your refrigerator.

6. Place cold mixture into the ice cream freezer and freeze according to manufacturer's directions.

**Variation:**

Use 1 cup of finely crumbled amaretto cookies. When ice cream is frozen, remove from ice cream machine and place in a clean container, and stir in the crumbled cookies. Put the frozen ice cream in the freezer for several hours before serving.

# Dulce de Leche Ice Cream

3 egg yolks

1 cup whole milk

1 (14-oz.) can sweetened condensed milk

3 cups light cream

2 cups Dulce de Leche liqueur

| **Yield:** 2 quarts |
| --- |
| **Prep time:** 40 minutes |
| **Cook time:** 20 minutes |

1. In a mixing bowl beat eggs until light and fluffy.

2. In the top of a double boiler over medium heat, combine the eggs and milk. Cook until temperature reaches 160°F (coats back of spoon). Remove from heat and place in an ice bath.

3. When mixture is cool, pour into a mixing bowl and add light cream and the Dulce de Leche liqueur. Mix well.

4. Cool mixture to 40°F in your refrigerator.

5. Place cold mixture into the ice cream freezer and freeze according to manufacturer's directions.

# White Crème de Menthe Ice Cream

4 egg yolks

1 cup table sugar

2 cups whole milk

¾ cup crème de menthe

3 cups light cream

3 cups whipping cream

| **Yield:** About 2 quarts |
| --- |
| **Prep time:** 40 minutes |
| **Cook time:** 15 minutes |

1. Beat eggs with sugar until light and fluffy.

2. In the top of a double boiler over medium heat, combine egg mixture and whole milk. Cook until temperature reaches 160°F (coats back of spoon). Remove from heat and place in an ice bath.

3. In a mixing bowl combine crème de menthe, light cream, whipping cream, and cooled egg mixture. Mix well.

4. Cool mixture to 40°F in your refrigerator.

5. Place cold mixture into the ice cream freezer and freeze according to manufacturer's directions.

# Margarita Ice Cream

5 egg yolks

1 (14-oz.) can sweetened
condensed milk

2 cups light cream

⅓ cup semisweetened lime juice

Zest from 1 lime

¼ cup tequila (or to taste)

2 TB. Cointreau liqueur (or any
orange-flavored liqueur)

**Yield:** About 2 quarts

**Prep time:** 45 minutes

**Cook time:** 25 minutes

1. In a mixing bowl beat egg yolks until light and fluffy.

2. In the top of the double boiler over medium heat, combine the eggs and lime zest with 2 cups light cream. Cook until temperature reaches 160°F (coats back of spoon). Remove from heat and place in an ice bath.

3. In a mixing bowl add condensed milk, lime juice, tequila, and 2 tablespoons Cointreau liqueur, and mix well.

4. Combine egg mixture with cream mixture and mix well.

5. Cool mixture to 40°F in your refrigerator.

6. Place cold mixture into the ice cream freezer and freeze according to manufacturer's directions.

# Piña Colada Ice Cream

1 TB. unflavored gelatin (1 oz.)

½ cup warm water

1 (12-oz.) can pineapple concentrate

1 (15-oz.) can cream of coconut

1½ cups dark rum

1 cup heavy cream

2 cups whipping cream

| | |
|---|---|
| **Yield:** About 2 quarts | |
| **Prep time:** 25 minutes | |
| **Cook time:** None | |

1. Dissolve gelatin in warm water and allow to sit until completely dehydrated (10 to 15 minutes).

2. In a blender place pineapple concentrate and cream of coconut, and set gelatin. Blend until gelatin is combined.

3. Place the pineapple, coconut, gelatin mixture, rum, heavy cream, and heavy cream in a mixing bowl and mix until well blended.

4. Cool mixture to 40°F in your refrigerator.

5. Place cold mixture into ice cream freezer and freeze according to manufacturer's instructions.

# Eggnog Ice Cream

6 egg yolks

1 cup table sugar

2 cups whole milk

1 (12-oz.) can evaporated milk

½ tsp. nutmeg

¾ tsp. cinnamon

3 cups whipping cream

4 TB. brandy

| |
|---|
| **Yield:** About 2 quarts |
| **Prep time:** 40 minutes |
| **Cook time:** 20 minutes |

1. Place egg yolks in a mixing bowl and beat until light and fluffy.

2. Blend cinnamon and nutmeg with sugar, and mix until well incorporated.

3. In the top of a double boiler over medium heat, combine the egg and whole milk mixtures and cook until temperature reaches 160°F (coats back of spoon). Remove from heat and place in an ice bath.

4. In a mixing bowl add egg mixture, evaporated milk, whipping cream, vanilla, and brandy. Mix well.

5. Cool mixture to 40°F in your refrigerator.

6. Place cold mixture in the ice cream freezer and freeze according to manufacturer's directions

# Crème de Cocoa Ice Cream

4 egg yolks

2⅓ cup table sugar

2 cups whole milk

2 cups light cream

2 cups heavy cream

1 TB. vanilla extract

1 cup crème de cocoa liqueur

**Yield:** About 2 quarts

**Prep time:** 40 minutes

**Cook time:** 20 minutes

1. Beat eggs and sugar until light and fluffy.

2. In the top of a double boiler over medium heat, combine the egg mixture and milk. Cook until temperature reaches 160°F (coats back of spoon). Remove from heat and place in an ice bath.

3. In a mixing bowl add light cream, heavy cream, vanilla extract, crème de cocoa, and cooled egg mixture. Mix until thoroughly blended.

4. Cool mixture to 40°F in your refrigerator.

5. Place cold mixture into the ice cream freezer and freeze according to manufacturer's directions.

# Rum Raisin Ice Cream

4 egg yolks

1 cup table sugar

2 cups whole milk

1¾ cups dark rum

1 cup raisins

4 cups whipping cream

**Yield:** About 2 quarts

**Prep time:** 35 minutes

**Cook time:** 20 minutes

1. Soak the raisins overnight in dark rum.

2. Beat eggs and sugar until light and fluffy.

3. In the top of a double boiler over medium heat, combine egg mixture and milk. Cook until temperature reaches 160°F. (Do not boil.) Remove from heat and place in an ice bath.

4. Strain raisins, and save rum.

5. In a mixing bowl combine egg mixture with whipping cream and rum.

6. Cool mixture to 40°F in your refrigerator.

7. Place cold mixture into the ice cream freezer and follow manufacturer's directions. Just before ice cream is done, open the machine and add raisins; then continue freezing, or mix raisins into ice cream after removing it from the machine.

**Variation:**

1½ cup hazelnuts, chopped

# Irish Cream Ice Cream

3 egg yolks

1 cup table sugar

3 cups half-and-half

½ light brown sugar

2 cups heavy cream

1 cup Irish cream liqueur

**Yield:** About 2 quarts

**Prep time:** 40 minutes

**Cook time:** 20 minutes

1. In a mixing bowl beat eggs, table sugar, and brown sugar until light and fluffy.

2. In the top of a double boiler over medium heat, combine egg mixture with 2 cups of half-and-half. Cook until temperature reaches 160°F (coats back of spoon). Remove from heat and place in an ice bath.

3. Place cooled egg and sugar mixture in a mixing bowl and add remaining half-and-half, heavy cream, and Irish cream. Mix well.

4. Cool mixture to 40°F in your refrigerator.

5. Place cold mixture into the ice cream freezer and freeze according to manufacturer's directions.

# Grand Marnier Ice Cream

3 egg yolks

2 cups whole milk

¾ cup table sugar

1 cup orange juice

1 TB. orange peel

¾ cup Grand Marnier liqueur (or any other orange-flavored liqueur)

2 cups heavy cream

2 cups light cream

**Yield:** About 2 quarts

**Prep time:** 30 minutes

**Cook time:** 10 minutes

1. Beat eggs and sugar together until light and fluffy

2. In the top of a double boiler over medium heat, combine the egg mixture, milk, and orange peel. Cook until temperature reaches 160°F (coats back of spoon). Remove from heat and place in an ice bath.

3. In a mixing bowl combine orange juice, Grand Marnier liqueur, heavy cream, light cream, and egg mixture. Mix until well blended.

4. Cool mixture to 40°F in your refrigerator.

5. Place cold mixture into the ice cream freezer and freeze according to the manufacturer's directions.

# Vodka Ice Cream with Ginger

1 ½ TB. cornstarch

2 cups whole milk

1 cup table sugar

1 cup chopped candied ginger

1 cup vodka

3 cups heavy cream

2 cups whipping cream

| **Yield:** About 2 quarts |
| **Prep time:** 35 minutes |
| **Cook time:** 15 minutes |

1. In the top of a double boiler combine 1 cup whole milk, ginger candies, and cornstarch. Cook until mixture thickens.

2. Remove from heat and allow to cool.

3. In a mixing bowl combine sugar and milk, mixing until sugar is dissolved.

4. Add vodka, heavy cream, and whipping cream to the sugar and milk mixture, and then add cornstarch. Blend well.

5. Cool mixture to 40°F in your refrigerator.

6. Place cold mixture into the ice cream freezer and freeze according to manufacturer's directions.

# Chapter 8

# Unusual Flavor Recipes

## In This Chapter

- ☺ Trying new things can be fun
- ☺ The most unusual flavors
- ☺ Keeping an open mind to flavors

You know what they say—there's no accounting for taste. So you just never know what unique flavor some people might really love.

This chapter contains some rather unusual, and perhaps even a few strange, flavors. Many go back to the days when special "store-bought" flavorings were unavailable and/or to the farming days when people like my grandparents made ice cream with whatever was available or abundant during the seasons.

## Roots of Unusual Flavors

Through the years people who have made ice cream at home and in small ice cream shops have had fun with "what's available" along with vivid imaginations. For example, here in New England I've known shops that have actually sold the following ice cream flavors: lobster, clam, quince, root beer, mustard, horseradish, sauerkraut, greengage, and dill pickle (great for expectant mothers). I have also visited an ice cream shop that sold all vegetable flavors (organic, of course)—yes, beet, okra, cabbage, spinach, and corn.

### The Real Scoop

Speaking of unusual flavors, since one out of every five ice cream eaters shares the treat with their dog or cat, perhaps liver or tuna can be the next unusual flavors. But not at my shop. Actually, there are one or two ice cream companies that manufacture "pet friendly flavors," which are better for pets' health than people ice cream.

Today, the unusual, with the help of lots of mix-ins, often comes in the form of cute names like: polka mocha, cactus candy crunch, yankee doodle strudel, mountain mash mania, malted moo goo, fascinating fireballs, tasty trail tarts, and so on. The only downside for shop owners and employees is that customers need a lengthy explanation of the actual ingredients.

Experimenting with the unknown, I have come up with some special tastes, especially ones like Sweet Potato, Mince Meat, and Jalapeño. The unusual flavors have fewer variations, as the flavors carry their own individuality, but I am willing to bet that you, the reader, can think of certain nuts, ripples, or combinations to make them even more special.

Also, I'd strongly encourage you to keep an open mind when contemplating an unusual—and perhaps strange-sounding—flavor. What seems weird at first may soon become your new favorite flavor. You really never know if you'll like a specific flavor until you've tried it at least once. Sure, the idea of cucumber ice cream might not initially make your mouth water, but you might be pleasantly surprised.

# Tomato Ice Cream

1 ½ TB. cornstarch

1 cup whole milk

1 (22-oz.) jar tomato-basil pasta sauce

1 (6-oz.) can tomato purée

2 cups heavy cream

2 cups light cream

| **Yield:** 2 quarts |
| :---: |
| **Prep time:** 30 minutes |
| **Cook time:** 15 minutes |

1. In a double boiler or heavy saucepan place 1 cup whole milk with 1½ tablespoons cornstarch. Cook over medium heat, stirring constantly until mixture forms a soft paste.

2. Remove mixture from heat and place in an ice bath until cold to the touch. If lumpy when cold, strain through a sieve.

3. In a large mixing bowl combine tomato sauce, tomato purée, light cream, and heavy cream. Mix until smooth.

4. Add cornstarch mixture to tomato mixture and blend well.

5. Cool mixture to 40°F in your refrigerator.

6. Place cold mixture into the ice cream freezer and freeze according to manufacturer's directions.

# Cucumber Ice Cream

5 cups puréed English cucumber (peeled)

1½ TB. cornstarch

1 cup whole milk

¼ tsp. sea salt

¼ tsp. kelp seasoning

2 cups whipping cream

**Yield:** About 2 quarts

**Prep time:** 40 minutes

**Cook time:** 15 minutes

1. In a food processor or blender purée 3 long English cucumbers, peeled, or enough to make 5 cups.

2. In a double boiler or heavy sauce pan over medium heat, cook 1 cup milk with 1½ tablespoons cornstarch until mixture forms a thin paste.

3. Remove from heat and place in an ice bath until mixture is cold to the touch. If mixture is lumpy, pass it through a sieve.

4. In a large mixing bowl combine cucumber purée, sea salt, kelp seasoning, whipping cream, and cold cornstarch mixture. Mix until well incorporated.

5. Cool mixture to 40°F in your refrigerator.

6. Place cold mixture into the ice cream freezer and freeze according to manufacturer's directions.

# Carrot Ice Cream

4 cups puréed carrots (10 to 12 carrots depending on size)

1½ TB. cornstarch

1 cup whole milk

3 cups light cream

**Yield:** About 2 quarts

**Prep time:** 60 minutes

**Cook time:** 30 minutes

1. Cook carrots until tender.

2. Drain carrots and save ¼ cup liquid. Allow to cool.

3. In a double boiler or heavy saucepan over medium heat, cook whole milk and cornstarch until mixture forms a soft paste.

4. Remove cornstarch mixture from heat and allow to cool. If lumpy pass through a sieve.

5. Purée carrots in a food processor or blender, adding carrot water if needed.

6. In a mixing bowl combine carrots, cornstarch mixture, and light cream. Mix well.

7. Cool mixture to 40°F in your refrigerator.

8. Place cold mixture into the ice cream freezer and freeze according to manufacturer's directions.

**Variation:**

1½ cups raisins

# Corn Ice Cream

8 egg yolks

2 cups whole milk

2 (14¾-oz.) cans cream corn

2 cups whipping cream

2 cups half-and-half

| | |
|---|---|
| **Yield:** About 2 quarts | |
| **Prep time:** 40 minutes | |
| **Cook time:** 20 minutes | |

1. Beat egg yolks until light and frothy.

2. In the top of a double boiler over medium heat, combine eggs and milk. Cook until temperature reaches 160°F (coats back of spoon). Remove from heat and place in an ice bath.

3. In a large mixing bowl place the cream corn, whipping cream, and half-and–half and egg mixture. Mix well.

4. Cool mixture to 40°F in your refrigerator.

5. Place cold mixture into the ice cream freezer and freeze according to manufacturer's directions.

# Sweet Potato Ice Cream

5 or 6 sweet potatoes

3 egg yolks

¼ cup sugar

2 cups whole milk

½ cup pure maple syrup

2 cups whipping cream

**Yield:** About 2 quarts

**Prep time:** 40 minutes

**Cook time:** 20 minutes

1. Peel and cook 5 or 6 large sweet potatoes until soft (3 cups puréed).

2. In a blender or food processor purée the potatoes.

3. Allow sweet potatoes to cool.

4. Beat egg and sugar until light and fluffy.

5. In the top of a double boiler over medium heat, combine 1 cup whole milk with egg mixture. Cook until temperature reaches 160°F (coats back of spoon).

6. Remove from heat stir in maple syrup and place egg mixture in an ice bath.

7. In mixing bowl place puréed sweet potato, remaining milk, whipping cream, and cooled egg mixture. Blend well.

8. Cool mixture to 40°F in your refrigerator.

9. Place cold mixture into the ice cream freezer and freeze according to manufacturer's directions.

**Variation:**

1½ cups miniature marshmallows

# Mincemeat Ice Cream

4 egg yolks

2 cups milk

3 TB. arrowroot

½ cup pure honey

2½ cups cooked mincemeat (can be purchased in a supermarket)

2 cups light cream

2 cups heavy cream

1 TB. vanilla extract

**Yield:** About 2 quarts

**Prep time:** 40 minutes

**Cook time:** 15 minutes

1. Beat egg yolks until light and fluffy. Add honey, half-and-half, and arrowroot. Beat until thick and creamy.

2. In the top of a double boiler over medium heat, cook egg mixture until temperature reaches 160°F (coats back of spoon). Remove from heat and place in an ice bath.

3. In a mixing bowl combine light cream, heavy cream, vanilla extract, mincemeat, and the cooled egg mixture. Mix until thoroughly combined.

4. Cool mixture to 40°F in your refrigerator.

5. Pour cold mixture into the ice cream freezer and freeze according to manufacturer's directions.

# Garlic Ice Cream

6 egg yolks

1 TB. honey

1 cup table sugar

2 cups whole milk

2 cups half-and-half

3 cups light cream

1 TB. lemon juice

¼ cup puréed garlic

| **Yield:** About 2 quarts |
| **Prep time:** 45 minutes |
| **Cook time:** 20 minutes |

1. Beat egg yolks and sugar until light and fluffy.

2. In the top of a double boiler over medium heat, combine egg mixture and whole milk and cook until mixture reaches 160°F (coats back of spoon).

3. Remove egg mixture from heat, stir in honey and place in an ice bath.

4. In a mixing bowl combine half-and-half, light cream, lemon juice, puréed garlic, and cold egg mixture. Mix until well combined.

5. Cool mixture to 40°F in your refrigerator.

6. Place cold mixture into the ice cream freezer and freeze according to manufacturer's directions.

### Cool Tips

For the garlic in this recipe, I use chopped garlic from a jar and purée it in a blender with just a touch of half-and-half.

# Jalapeño Ice Cream

4 egg yolks

1 cup table sugar

3 cups half-and-half

4 cups light cream

1 (4-oz.) jar jalapeño peppers

**Yield:** About 2 quarts

**Prep time:** 45 minutes

**Cook time:** 20 minutes

1. In a blender purée jalapeño peppers with ¼ cup half-and-half.

2. Beat egg yolks and sugar until light and fluffy.

3. In the top of a double boiler over medium heat, combine egg mixture with 2 cups half-and–half. Cook until temperature reaches 160°F (coats back of spoon). Remove from heat and cool in an ice bath.

4. In a mixing bowl combine remaining half-and-half, light cream, cold egg mixture, and puréed jalapeños. Mix well.

5. Cool mixture to 40°F in your refrigerator.

6. Place cold mixture into the ice cream freezer and freeze according to manufacturer's directions.

# Molasses Ice Cream

2 cups molasses

3 cups heavy cream

3 cups half-and-half

| | |
|---|---|
| **Yield:** About 2 quarts | |
| **Prep time:** 15 minutes | |
| **Cook time:** None | |

1. Combine molasses, heavy cream, and half-and-half in a mixing bowl until well blended.

2. Cool mixture to 40°F in your refrigerator.

3. Place cold mixture into the ice cream freezer and freeze according to manufacturer's directions.

**Variations:**

1½ cups nuts, chopped

1½ cups cookie pieces

1½ cups chocolate bits

Ripples: marshmallow

# Oatmeal Ice Cream

1½ cups oatmeal (not instant)

3 TB. cornstarch

1 cup whole milk

1 (14-oz.) can sweetened condensed milk

2 cups light cream

3 cups whipping cream

1 TB. vanilla extract

| | |
|---|---|
| **Yield:** 2 quarts | |
| **Prep time:** 45 minutes | |
| **Cook time:** 30 minutes | |

1. Preheat oven to 350°F. Spread oatmeal on baking sheet and toast for up to 30 minutes. Shake and turn sheet several times (do not burn). Remove from oven and cool.

2. Place cornstarch and milk in a double boiler and cook until mixture thickens. Remove from heat and cool.

3. In a blender place oatmeal and light cream. Blend until oatmeal is finely ground (forms a thin paste).

4. Add cornstarch mixture to blender with condensed milk and blend until incorporated.

5. In a mixing bowl combine whipping cream, oatmeal mixture, and vanilla extract. Mix well.

6. Cool mixture to 40°F in your refrigerator.

7. Stir again before adding to the ice cream freezer.

8. Place cold mixture into the ice cream freezer and freeze according to manufacturer's directions.

**Variations:**

1½ cups oatmeal-raisin cookies

1½ cups chocolate or butterscotch bits

Ripples: maple syrup, fruit purées, etc.

# Tutti Frutti Ice Cream

2 TB. gelatin (2 oz.)

½ cup warm water

1 (9-oz.) can crushed pineapple

1 can pineapple frozen concentrate

1 large ripe banana

8 oz. dried cranberries

1 (8-oz.) jar pitted cherries

1 cup table sugar

1 can evaporated milk

3 cups half-and-half

2 cups light cream

**Yield:** About 2 quarts

**Prep time:** 25 minutes

**Cook time:** None

1. Dissolve gelatin in warm water until completely dehydrated (10 to 15 minutes).

2. In a blender add pineapple concentrate, crushed pineapple, banana, cranberries, and cherries with the sugar and 2 cups light cream. Blend until mixture contains small pieces of ingredients. Add gelatin and mix until incorporated (do not overblend).

3. In a mixing bowl add blender mixture, evaporated milk, and half-and–half. Mix well.

4. Cool mixture to 40°F in your refrigerator.

5. Place cold mixture into ice cream freezer and freeze according to manufacturer's instructions.

# Rose Petal Ice Cream

2 (1-oz.) packages gelatin

½ cup warm water

5 cups heavy cream

2 cups half-and-half

2 TB. rose water

**Yield:** About 2 quarts

**Prep time:** 20 minutes

**Cook time:** None

1. Add the 2 oz. gelatin to the warm water for 5 minutes or until gelatin is completely dissolved.

2. Place 1 cup half-and-half in a blender and add the dissolved gelatin. Blend until gelatin is incorporated with the half-and-half (no lumps). If lumps occur, strain through a sieve.

3. In a mixing bowl place the half-and-half, gelatin mixture, heavy cream, and rose water. Mix well.

4. Cool to 40°F.

5. Placed cooled mixture into your ice cream maker and follow the manufacturer's instructions.

# Part 3

# Other Frozen Delights

Not that I think you'd ever get tired of ice cream, but there are many other wonderful desserts in the ice cream family that you can try. In this section, I'll share many recipes for making your own sherbets and sorbets (and, yes, I'll explain the difference). As yogurt is really popular right now, I'll give you some recipes for making tasty variations. Then I'll tell you all about gelato and show you how to make several different types.

# Chapter **9**

# Sherbet

## In This Chapter

- ☺ How sherbet differs from ice cream
- ☺ Special steps for making sherbet
- ☺ A handy simple syrup recipe

Sherbet is similar to ice cream, in that it's also a sweet and delicious frozen treat. But sherbet has some special qualities that set it apart from ice cream. According to FDA standards of identity, sherbets must have a milkfat content of not less than 1 nor more than 2 percent. Their sweetener content is also slightly higher than that of ice cream. Sherbet is usually flavored with fruit or sometimes other ingredients that provide a characteristically sherbet type of flavor. Sherbet is also the next most popular dessert after ice cream.

## Tips for Making Sherbet

There are some special things you need to consider when making sherbet using an ice and rock salt ice cream freezer. First, you have to change the ratio of salt to ice. You now have to use one part salt to six parts ice. Because of all the extra sugar, sherbet may need a colder temperature to freeze than ice cream does.

### The Real Scoop

The Chinese are generally given credit for first creating sherbet, but other cultures such as Turkey and Persia can trace sherbet roots back to them. Today, people all over the world enjoy this tasty treat.

To soften a sherbet to a serving consistency, either microwave it briefly (15 to 30 seconds) or put it in the refrigerator for a while before serving.

When storing sherbet, it will keep at a serving temperature better if kept in the freezer part of your refrigerator as the temperature in your refrigerator freezer is higher than in your chest freezer.

# Simple Syrup Recipe

I have a quick, simple syrup recipe that can be used in the recipes in this and other chapters:

1. Mix 2½ pounds table sugar with 1 quart water.

2. Place the water and sugar in a heavy saucepan, stir until mixture comes to a boil and sugar is dissolved.

3. Cool completely before using.

### The Real Scoop

Originally European sherbets just included a beaten white egg, but the Americanized version today has milk or cream.

# Lemon Sherbet

2 cups corn syrup

1 (12-oz.) can frozen lemon concentrate

5 cups whole milk

Pinch of salt

**Yield:** About 2 quarts

**Prep time:** 20 minutes

**Cook time:** None

1. In a mixing bowl add the cold corn syrup, lemon concentrate, milk, and salt.

2. Stir the mixture until thoroughly blended.

3. Cool mixture to 40°F in your refrigerator.

4. Place cold mixture into the ice cream freezer and freeze according to manufacturer's instructions.

# Apple Sherbet

1 (12-oz.) container apple concentrate

1½ cups simple syrup

3 cups evaporated milk

2 cups whole milk

**Yield:** About 2 quarts

**Prep time:** 10 minutes

**Cook time:** None

1. In a mixing bowl, blend together apple concentrate, simple syrup, evaporated milk, and whole milk.

2. Cool mixture to 40°F in your refrigerator.

3. Place cold mixture into the ice cream freezer and freeze according to manufacturer's instructions.

## The Real Scoop

In Europe, the term sherbet is also used in reference to a sweet candy powder. It's often sold in a straw, made from licorice or other candy.

# Coffee Sherbet

1 cup of water

2 TB. cornstarch

1 cup simple syrup

¾ cup instant coffee

5 cups half-and-half

| **Yield:** About 2 quarts |
| :--- |
| **Prep time:** 15 minutes |
| **Cook time:** 7 minutes |

1. In the top of a double boiler over medium heat, place 1 cup water with 2 tablespoons cornstarch. Cook until mixture thickens. Remove from heat and place in an ice bath until cold.

2. In a mixing bowl combine simple syrup, half-and-half, instant coffee, and cold cornstarch mixture. Mix until well blended (no lumps). If mixture is lumpy, strain through a sieve.

3. Cool mixture to 40°F in your refrigerator.

4. Place cold mixture into the ice cream freezer and freeze according to manufacturer's instructions.

## Avoid a Meltdown

If you travel overseas, don't be surprised when you order a sherbet if you receive something other than sherbet. Overseas, sherbet can be a slang term for various nondessert items. In Australia, for example, sherbet is an old slang term for beer.

# Orange Sherbet

1 (11-oz.) can mandarin oranges

1 (12-oz.) can orange juice concentrate

2 cups table sugar

5 cups whole milk

4 TB. lemon juice

| **Yield:** About 2 quarts |
| **Prep time:** 10 minutes |
| **Cook time:** None |

1. Strain juice from mandarin oranges and purée oranges in a blender.

2. In a mixing bowl combine puréed mandarin oranges, orange juice concentrate, sugar, milk, and lemon juice. Mix well.

3. Cool mixture to 40°F in your refrigerator.

4. Place cold mixture into the ice cream freezer and freeze according to manufacturer's instructions.

# White Grape Sherbet

1 TB. unflavored gelatin (1 oz.)

1 (11-oz.) can white grape juice concentrate

1 cup warm water

5 cups whole milk

| **Yield:** About 2 quarts |
| **Prep time:** 10 minutes |
| **Cook time:** None |

1. Mix gelatin in 1 cup water until completely dissolved.

2. In a mixing bowl combine grape concentrate and gelatin, and mix until gelatin is incorporated. (If gelatin will not incorporate, then place in a blender and mix.)

3. Add milk and mix well.

4. Cool mixture to 40°F in your refrigerator.

5. Place cold mixture into the ice cream freezer and freeze according to manufacturer's instructions.

**The Real Scoop**

Sherbet became popular in this country around 1932, during the Depression, when cream products where in short supply. That was also the situation during World War II.

# Tea Sherbet

2 TB. cornstarch

2 cups water

1½ cups unsweetened tea powder

¾ cups table sugar

4 cups milk

**Yield:** About 2 quarts

**Prep time:** 10 minutes

**Cook time:** None

1. In the top of a double boiler place 1 cup water with 2 tablespoons cornstarch. Cook over medium heat until mixture thickens. Remove from heat and place in an ice bath.

2. In a mixing bowl combine the second cup water, unsweetened tea powder, sugar, and milk. Mix well.

3. Cool mixture to 40°F in your refrigerator.

4. Place cold mixture into the ice cream freezer and freeze according to manufacturer's instructions.

 **The Real Scoop**

Sherbet was the name of a popular Australian pop group in the 1970s.

# Peach Sherbet

5–6 peaches (4 cups puréed)
1 cup water
1 cup table sugar
3 cups half-and-half

**Yield:** About 2 quarts

**Prep time:** 10 minutes

**Cook time:** None

1. Wash peaches and remove pits (do not peel).

2. In a blender, purée peaches until smooth. If the mixture is lumpy, pass it through a sieve.

3. In a mixing bowl combine puréed peaches, sugar, half-and-half, and the water. Mix until sugar is dissolved.

4. Cool mixture to 40°F in your refrigerator.

5. Place cold mixture into the ice cream freezer and freeze according to manufacturer's instructions.

# Apricot Sherbet

10–12 apricots (4 cups puréed)
1½ cups corn syrup
1 cup water
2 cups milk

**Yield:** About 2 quarts

**Prep time:** 10 minutes

**Cook time:** None

1. Wash and pit apricots.

2. In a blender purée apricots until smooth. If mixture is lumpy, pass through a sieve.

3. In a mixing bowl combine puréed apricots, corn syrup, water, and milk. Mix well.

4. Cool mixture to 40°F in your refrigerator.

5. Place cold mixture into the ice cream freezer and freeze according to manufacturer's instructions.

# Cranberry Sherbet

2 (16-oz.) cans whole cranberry sauce

4 egg whites

1 cup water

2 cups whole milk

2 TB. lemon juice

| |
|---|
| **Yield:** About 2 quarts |
| **Prep time:** 10 minutes |
| **Cook time:** None |

1. In a blender purée whole cranberry sauce until smooth. Strain mixture through a sieve.

2. Beat egg whites until stiff (use copper, glass, or plastic mixing bowl).

3. In a mixing bowl add cranberry purée, water, milk, and lemon juice. Mix well.

4. Slowly add egg whites until thoroughly incorporated.

5. Cool mixture to 40°F in your refrigerator.

6. Place cold mixture into the ice cream freezer and freeze according to manufacturer's instructions.

# Strawberry Sherbet

2 (16-oz.) pkgs. frozen unsweetened strawberries (thawed)

2 cups water

1 cup simple syrup

1 cup whole milk

| |
|---|
| **Yield:** About 2 quarts |
| **Prep time:** 10 minutes |
| **Cook time:** None |

1. In a blender purée strawberries with the water.

2. In a mixing bowl combine the puréed strawberries with the simple syrup and milk. Mix well.

3. Cool in refrigerator to 40°F.

4. Place cold mixture into the ice cream freezer and freeze according to manufacturer's instructions.

# Pineapple Sherbet

1 TB. unflavored gelatin (1 oz.)

2 (16-oz.) pkgs. frozen unsweetened pineapple

2 cups water

½ cup table sugar

2 cups milk

| | |
|---|---|
| **Yield:** About 2 quarts | |
| **Prep time:** 10 minutes | |
| **Cook time:** None | |

1. Mix gelatin with 1 cup water and allow to sit until completely dissolved (10 to 15 minutes).

2. In a blender purée pineapple with 1 cup water and sugar.

3. In a mixing bowl combine pineapple and gelatin and mix to blend. If mixture has lumps, strain through a sieve.

4. In a mixing bowl place pineapple and gelatin mixture and add milk. Mix well.

5. Cool mixture to 40°F in your refrigerator.

6. Place cold mixture into the ice cream freezer and freeze according to manufacturer's instructions.

## Blueberry Sherbet

2 (16-oz.) packages
unsweetened blueberries

2 cups water

1 cup table sugar

1 TB. cornstarch

1 cup half-and-half

**Yield:** About 2 quarts

**Prep time:** 10 minutes

**Cook time:** 10 minutes

1. In a blender, purée blueberries with 1 cup water and sugar.

2. In the top of a double boiler place 1 cup water with 1 tablespoon cornstarch. Cook over medium heat, stirring constantly, until mixture thickens. Remove from heat and place in an ice bath until cool to the touch.

3. In a mixing bowl, mix blueberry/sugar mixture with cooled cornstarch and half-and-half. Mix well.

4. Cool mixture to 40°F in your refrigerator.

5. Place cold mixture into the ice cream freezer and freeze according to manufacturer's instructions.

## Black Raspberry Sherbet

2 (16-oz.) pkg. frozen black raspberries

2 cups water

1½ cups simple syrup

1 cup light cream

**Yield:** About 2 quarts

**Prep time:** 10 minutes

**Cook time:** None

1. In a blender purée raspberries with 1 cup water.

2. In a mixing bowl combine raspberry purée, 1 cup water, simple syrup, and light cream. Mix well.

3. Cool mixture to 40°F in your refrigerator.

4. Place cold mixture into the ice cream freezer and freeze according to manufacturer's instructions.

# Cherry Sherbet

2 (13-oz.) jars cherry preserves

3 cups water

2 cups milk

**Yield:** About 2 quarts

**Prep time:** 10 minutes

**Cook time:** None

1. In a blender combine cherry preserves with 2 cups water and blend until smooth.

2. In a mixing bowl, add remaining water and milk to cherry preserve mixture. Mix well.

3. Cool mixture to 40°F in your refrigerator.

4. Place cold mixture into the ice cream freezer and freeze according to manufacturer's instructions.

# Cantaloupe Sherbet

4 cantaloupes, peeled and seeded (6 cups puree)

1 cup water

1 cup whole milk

1 TB. lemon juice

**Yield:** About 2 quarts

**Prep time:** 20 minutes

**Cook time:** None

1. In a blender purée cantaloupe. Continue to add pulp until you get 6 cups purée.

2. In a mixing bowl combine puréed cantaloupe, water, milk, and lemon juice. Mix well.

3. Cool mixture to 40°F in your refrigerator.

4. Place the mixture into the ice cream freezer and freeze according to manufacturer's instructions.

# Pear Sherbet

5–6 Barlett pears, peeled and seeded (6 cups puree)
½ cup table sugar
1 cup whole milk
1 TB. lemon juice

**Yield:** About 2 quarts

**Prep time:** 20 minutes

**Cook time:** None

1. In a blender purée pears. Add sugar and blend until sugar is dissolved.

2. In a mixing bowl combine pear purée, milk, and lemon juice.

3. Cool mixture to 40°F in your refrigerator.

4. Place cold mixture into the ice cream freezer and freeze according to manufacturer's instructions.

# Watermelon Sherbet

½ seedless watermelon
½ cup table sugar
1½ cups whole milk

**Yield:** About 2 quarts

**Prep time:** 20 minutes

**Cook time:** None

1. Scoop out pulp from watermelon and place in a blender. Continue to add pulp until you get 6 cups purée.

2. In a blender add sugar to purée and blend until sugar is dissolved.

3. Pour mixture into a mixing bowl and add milk. Mix well.

4. Cool mixture to 40°F in your refrigerator.

5. Place cold mixture into the ice cream freezer and freeze according to manufacturer's instructions.

# Chapter

# Sorbet

## In This Chapter

- ☺ What you won't find in a sorbet
- ☺ How syrup affects sorbet's flavor
- ☺ The difference between sherbet and sorbet

Sorbet is similar to sherbet, but is made using no dairy ingredients. In European countries, sorbet was traditionally served between courses of a meal to give people a chance to "cleanse their palate."

Sorbets as well as sherbets are great palate cleansers because they are lighter than ice cream and have a higher freezing point. The sorbet cleanses the palate by rinsing the surface of the tongue, and the citric acid of the fruit helps cause the gastric juices to flow. It is at that point when you are ready to taste more food.

A sorbet's appeal to many is that it has no cholesterol, is dairy free, and has a lower calorie count. Many connoisseurs of sorbet feel that they must be made with fresh fruit, and that they should have a small amount of similar or matching liqueur flavor.

For example, Grand Marnier would be used to boost the flavor of an orange sorbet. But remember that alcohol slows the freezing process.

I have found that it is easier to achieve a stronger flavor in sorbet than in a sherbet, even using the same ingredients, because of the absence of dairy. Most sorbets are inexpensive and simple to prepare.

Sorbets are also called water ices, Italian ices, fruit ices, flavored ices, and sometimes *granitas*. Sorbet is a mixture of frozen fruit purées and sugar syrup, occasionally with liquor added. *Granita* in Italian means "grain" and *granitas*, similarly to the sorbet, are a combination of fruits, ice, and a sweetener.

## Sorbet Tips

Just as with sherbet, if you are using an ice and rock salt freezer you must adjust the ratio of salt to ice when making sorbet. Likewise, sorbet will store better in the freezer section of the refrigerator, as opposed to the colder chest freezer.

The density of the sugar syrup affects the texture of a sorbet. French sorbets use lighter syrup and have a more grainy texture. Italian sorbets, which use heavier syrup, have a smoother texture.

# Cantaloupe Sorbet

2 large cantaloupes (6 cups puréed)

⅔ cup table sugar

½ cup orange juice

2 tsp. lemon juice

**Yield:** About 2 quarts

**Prep time:** 20 minutes

**Cook time:** None

1. Peel and seed cantaloupe. Place cantaloupe in a blender and purée until you get 6 cups of cantaloupe.

2. In a mixing bowl add cantaloupe, sugar, orange juice, and lemon juice and mix well.

3. Cool mixture to 40°F in your refrigerator.

4. Place cold mixture into the ice cream freezer and freeze according to manufacturer's instructions.

# Mango Sorbet

4–5 ripe mangos (4 cups puréed)
1 TB. unflavored gelatin (1 oz.)
¼ cup cold water
¾ cup boiling water
1 cup table sugar
2 TB. lemon juice

**Yield:** About 2 quarts

**Prep time:** 20 minutes

**Cook time:** 10 minutes

1. Peel and seed mangos and place pulp in a blender. Continue to add pulp until you get 4 cups purée.

2. Place the gelatin in cold water and allow to sit until completely dehydrated.

3. In a saucepan boil ¾ cup water. Remove from heat.

4. Add the dissolved gelatin and sugar to the hot water and stir until sugar is dissolved. Remove from heat and cool to room temperature.

5. In a mixing bowl combine mango purée and cooled gelatin/sugar/water mixture. Add lemon juice and stir until well mixed.

6. Cool mixture to 40°F in your refrigerator.

7. Place cold mixture into the ice cream freezer and freeze according to manufacturer's instructions for making sorbet.

# Cherry Sorbet

1 lb. cherries (4 cups puréed)

2 cups table sugar

1 cup water

1 tsp. lemon juice

| | |
|---|---|
| **Yield:** About 2 quarts | |
| **Prep time:** 20 minutes | |
| **Cook time:** 8 minutes | |

1. Place pitted ripe cherries in a blender. Continue to add cherries until you get 4 cups purée.

2. In a heavy saucepan combine sugar and water. Heat and stir until sugar is dissolved. Remove from heat and cool to room temperature.

3. In a mixing bowl combine cherry purée and lemon juice. Add cool sugar and mix well.

4. Cool mixture to 40°F in your refrigerator.

5. Place cold mixture into the ice cream freezer and freeze according to manufacturer's instructions for making sorbet.

## The Real Scoop

Because it is made without any dairy products, sorbet is often a popular ice cream alternative for vegetarians and others who avoid animal-related foods, or for people who can't tolerate dairy products.

# Lemon Sorbet

10–15 lemons (4 cups fresh
squeezed lemon juice
3 TB. lemon zest
2 cups table sugar (or to taste)
1 cup water

| Yield: About 2 quarts |
| :--- |
| **Prep time:** 10 minutes |
| **Cook time:** 20 minutes |

1. If you are using fresh lemons, roll one at a time on the counter under heavy palm pressure to soften lemon and make it easier to juice.

2. Zest several lemons to get 3 tablespoons.

3. Cut lemons in half and squeeze juice from them.

4. In a heavy saucepan combine sugar and water. Heat and stir until sugar is dissolved. Remove from heat and cool to room temperature.

5. In a mixing bowl combine lemon juice, lemon zest, and sugar water. Mix well.

6. Cool mixture to 40°F in your refrigerator.

7. Place cold mixture into the ice cream freezer and freeze according to manufacturer's instructions for making sorbet.

# Fresh Dill Sorbet

4 cups water

2 cups table sugar

¾ cup fresh dill (with stems)

½ cup lemon juice

½ cup light rum

**Yield:** About 2 quarts

**Prep time:** 30 minutes

**Cook time:** 20 minutes

1. In a heavy saucepan combine sugar and water. Heat and stir until sugar is dissolved.

2. Lower the heat to medium and add dill with stems to sugar water. Simmer for 15 to 20 minutes. Remove from heat and strain mixture through a sieve. Cool to room temperature.

3. In a mixing bowl combine cool sugar/water/dill mixture, lemon juice, and light rum. Mix well.

4. Cool mixture to 40°F in your refrigerator.

5. Place the cold mixture into the ice cream freezer and freeze according to manufacturer's instructions for making sorbet.

# Cucumber Sorbet

4–6 English cucumbers (5 cups purée)

2 TB. lemon juice

1½ cups simple syrup

1 cup water

**Yield:** About 2 quarts

**Prep time:** 15 minutes

**Cook time:** None

1. Peel and cube cucumber and place in a blender. Continue to add until you get 5 cups purée.

2. In a mixing bowl add cucumber purée, lemon juice, simple syrup, and water. Mix well.

3. Cool mixture to 40°F in your refrigerator.

4. Place cold mixture into the ice cream freezer and freeze according to manufacturer's instructions for making sorbet.

# Chocolate Sorbet

7 oz. semisweet baking chocolate

4 cups water

2 cups simple syrup

1 TB. crème de cocoa liqueur

| | |
|---|---|
| **Yield:** About 2 quarts | |
| **Prep time:** 15 minutes | |
| **Cook time:** 10 minutes | |

1. In a double boiler over medium heat melt semisweet chocolate.

2. When chocolate is melted, stir in 1 cup at a time the 4 cups hot water. Stir until chocolate is totally incorporated. Remove from heat.

3. In a mixing bowl combine chocolate mixture with simple syrup and crème de cocoa. Mix well.

4. Cool mixture to 40°F in your refrigerator.

5. Place cold mixture into the ice cream freezer and freeze according to manufacturer's instructions for making sorbet.

## Orange Banana Pineapple Sorbet

2 (12-oz.) cans orange banana pineapple concentrate (3 cups thawed)

4 cups water

½ cup simple syrup

| |
|---|
| **Yield:** About 2 quarts |
| **Prep time:** 10 minutes |
| **Cook time:** None |

1. In a mixing bowl combine thawed concentrate, water, and simple syrup. Mix well.

2. Cool mixture to 40°F in your refrigerator.

3. Place cold mixture into the ice cream freezer and freeze according to manufacturer's instructions for making sorbet.

### Cool Tips

By following the recipe above, you can make any frozen fruit concentrate found in your local supermarket, such as apple, cherry, orange, grapefruit, grape (both white and red), cranberry, ice tea, lime, lemon, orange-pineapple-apple, strawberry, lemonade, berry sun splash, and many others. This recipe has a strong flavor, which I like, but you may want to reduce the concentrate to your taste.

## Pomegranate Sorbet

½ cup pomegranate juice concentrate

5 cups water

2 cups simple syrup

| |
|---|
| **Yield:** About 2 quarts |
| **Prep time:** 10 minutes |
| **Cook time:** None |

1. In a mixing bowl combine pomegranate concentrate, water, and simple syrup. Mix well.

2. Cool mixture to 40°F in your refrigerator.

3. Place cold mixture into the ice cream freezer and freeze according to manufacturer's instructions for making sorbet.

# Hazelnut Sorbet

1 (12.7-oz.) bottle hazelnut
flavoring syrup

4 cups water

1 cup simple syrup

1 TB. Frangelico liqueur
(optional)

| | |
|---|---|
| **Yield:** About 2 quarts | |
| **Prep time:** 10 minutes | |
| **Cook time:** None | |

1. In a mixing bowl combine the hazelnut syrup, water, simple syrup, and Frangelico liqueur. Mix well.

2. Cool mixture to 40°F in your refrigerator.

3. Place the cold mixture into the ice cream freezer and freeze according to manufacturer's instructions for making sorbet.

# Plum Wine Sorbet

16–17 ripe plums (3 cups puréed)

2 cups Zinfandel wine

1 cup water

1 cup table sugar

| | |
|---|---|
| **Yield:** About 2 quarts | |
| **Prep time:** 20 minutes | |
| **Cook time:** None | |

1. Place peeled and pitted ripe plums in a blender. Continue to add plums until you get 3 cups purée. Add sugar and blend until sugar is dissolved.

2. In a mixing bowl, add plum/ sugar purée to water and Zinfandel wine. Mix well.

3. Cool mixture to 40°F in your refrigerator.

4. Place cold mixture into the ice cream freezer and freeze according to manufacturer's instructions for making sorbet.

# Tomato Basil Sorbet

4½ cups tomato sauce with basil

3 TB. lemon juice

1½ cups water

1½ cups simple syrup

**Yield:** About 2 quarts

**Prep time:** 20 minutes

**Cook time:** None

1. In a mixing bowl combine the tomato sauce, lemon juice, water, and simple syrup. Mix well.

2. Cool mixture to 40°F in your refrigerator.

3. Place cold mixture into the ice cream freezer and freeze according to manufacturer's instructions for making sorbet.

# Rhubarb Sorbet

12 long stalks of rhubarb (1½ pints puréed)

2½ cups water

1½ cups table sugar

¾ cup rhubarb syrup

**Yield:** About 2 quarts

**Prep time:** 45 minutes

**Cook time:** 20 minutes

1. Remove all leaves and ends from rhubarb stocks, cut into small pieces, and steam over 2½ cups water until soft.

2. Remove rhubarb from heat and purée in a blender. (Save steam water.)

3. In a saucepan combine steam water and sugar, and cook over high heat until liquid is reduced to about 1¼ cups liquid.

4. Remove from heat and cool in an ice bath.

5. When the syrup mixture is cool to the touch, place in a mixing bowl and add rhubarb purée. Mix well.

6. Cool mixture to 40°F in your refrigerator.

7. Place cold mixture into the ice cream freezer and freeze according to manufacturer's instructions for making sorbet.

# Root Beer Sorbet

1 TB. unflavored gelatin (1 oz.)

½ cup water

½ cup simple syrup

4 (12-oz.) cans root beer

1 TB. root beer extract

**Yield:** About 2 quarts

**Prep time:** 15 minutes

**Cook time:** 10 minutes

1. In a mixing bowl, combine gelatin and water and let sit until completely dehydrated (10 to 15 minutes).

2. Pour gelatin into a saucepan and over low heat stir until gelatin is dissolved.

3. In a mixing bowl combine gelatin mixture, simple syrup, root beer, and root beer extract. Mix well.

4. Cool mixture to 40°F in your refrigerator.

5. Place cold mixture into the ice cream freezer and freeze according to manufacturer's instructions for making sorbet.

# Chapter 11

# Yogurt

## In This Chapter

- ☺ Yogurt's living ingredients
- ☺ The pros and cons of yogurt
- ☺ The right way to drain whey

For clarification purposes please note: the recipes in this section all require taking plain soft store-bought "yogurt" and transforming it with the aid of flavorings and the same freezing process as ice cream into a finished frozen product we will call "frozen yogurt."

It is difficult to talk about yogurt as a frozen dessert without first discussing yogurt in its original form. Yogurt was introduced into this country, it is believed, by European and Asian immigrants who had made and eaten yogurtlike products for years. Brewing sour fermented milk for drinking was part of their culture. Around that time a Russian by the name of E. Metchnikov in 1908 referred in his book to "prolongation of life," feeling that the brew of yogurt that mountain dwellers drank helped longevity. There has been much debate over that issue through the years but the science of probotics has now shown evidence that foods containing live bacteria are good for our health.

However, it wasn't until the late 1970s, and continuing throughout the fitness-crazed 1980s, that yogurt enjoyed a popularity boom. Most of us are familiar with yogurt, but do you really know what it is? Yogurt is a dessert (or snack) food consisting of a combination of milk and other dairy products, which have been cultured, plus ingredients added for sweetening and flavor.

By definition, yogurt must contain cultures. These are tiny living organisms, which may sound a bit scary, but they're actually good for you. They are believed to help improve the body's immune system, and can also encourage the growth of "good" bacteria, which help fight infections.

Yogurt is also a great source of calcium, protein, and other things your body needs. And as such, yogurt is popular with people who are interested in health and fitness. Evidence has shown that yogurt must be eaten regularly to be effective. A steady supply of the yogurt culture in the body means that the yogurt bacteria are present in the intestines where they can be a benefit.

> **Avoid a Meltdown**
>
> Yogurt is generally low in fat, cholesterol, and sodium, but it is high in sugar and often calories.

## Yogurt Shops vs. Make-at-Home

Because of limited space, with all the flavors that ice cream shops like to sell, frozen yogurt flavors are usually limited or served from multi-flavored soft-serve machines. For example, my shop, Four Seas Ice Cream, does not have a yogurt flavor that duplicates any of my ice cream flavors. I also make frozen yogurt in a batch freezer and scoop it just like ice cream.

> **The Real Scoop**
>
> The impression exists in some minds that yogurt is made from stale milk that dairies cannot use. Nothing could be further from the truth, as yogurt is made from fresh high-quality milk.

At home, however, you can go wild with choices, including those tailored to your special tastes and dietary lifestyle. But remember, the lower the fat you use, the more creaminess you will lose. At home you can keep flavors tart or make them sweeter, and you can adjust cholesterol, carbohydrates, and calorie content. Fruit flavors seem to be the most popular but your flavor choices are endless.

In this book, I have tried to pick out potential favorites, and a few unusual flavors. Because yogurt contains a bacteria-driven culture, and the formulas can be time-consuming, I have chosen to use recipes that start with store-bought "plain" yogurt. Try to purchase those labeled "contains active yogurt cultures," whether regular or low fat. Whole milk yogurt and organic yogurt tend to be the best for homemade frozen yogurt recipes.

# Yogurt-Making Basics

When preparing frozen yogurt, I like to first drain some of the liquid (whey) out of it by placing a damp cheesecloth over a bowl and pouring the yogurt into it. You can also use a sieve or colander over a bowl but I prefer the cheesecloth, as it is easier to work with. Placing the yogurt in the refrigerator to drain for about ½ hour will give you the best results. You don't have to drain the whey, but this process gives a creamier texture to the yogurt.

You can save the whey that you drained and use it to make high-protein sorbets or ices. (Just use the whey in place of some of the water.) Making frozen yogurt is relatively easy, using just a few ingredients, and you can make a delicious dessert.

In all of the recipes that follow I have strained the yogurt in cheese cloth over a bowl in the refrigerator for ½ hour to remove some of the whey.

## The Real Scoop

As you will see, I have added milk or cream in a few of the recipes. Some people call this "yogurt ice cream," but I feel that as there are no government standards on how to make frozen yogurt, adding milk or cream will not change the name.

# Raspberry Yogurt

2 cups raspberry purée (12 oz. fresh or frozen)

½ cup corn syrup

¼ cup table sugar

2 cups plain yogurt

**Yield:** About 1 quart

**Prep time:** 10 minutes

**Cook time:** None

1. In a blender or food processor purée raspberries.

2. Strain raspberries thru a sieve and return to food processor or blender.

3. Add corn syrup, plain yogurt, and sugar to puréed raspberry and blend until incorporated.

4. Cool mixture to 40°F in your refrigerator.

5. Place cold mixture into the ice cream freezer and freeze according to the manufacturer's directions for making yogurt.

# Lime Yogurt

1 cup lime concentrate

⅔ cup table sugar

2¼ cups plain yogurt

**Yield:** About 1 quart

**Prep time:** 10 minutes

**Cook time:** None

1. In a blender or food processor blend lime concentrate and sugar.

2. Place yogurt in a mixing bowl and add the lime/sugar mixture. Mix well (no lumps).

3. Cool mixture to 40°F in your refrigerator.

4. Place cold mixture into the ice cream freezer and freeze according to manufacturer's instructions for making yogurt.

 **The Real Scoop**

Using this recipe you can make any of the frozen concentrates into a yogurt. We suggest that you taste the mixture as you might want to adjust the sweetness.

# Honey Yogurt

3 cups plain yogurt

1 cup honey

| **Yield:** About 1 quart |
| --- |
| **Prep time:** 10 minutes |
| **Cook time:** None |

1. In a mixing bowl combine yogurt and honey. Mix well until smooth (no lumps).

2. Cool mixture to 40°F in your refrigerator.

3. Place cold mixture into the ice cream freezer and freeze according to manufacturer's instructions for making yogurt.

## Cool Tips

When serving yogurt I have found that no more than 1 to 2 hours of freezing are necessary, if any at all. Most of the recipes can be eaten right out of the ice cream freezer. If you are using a deep freezer to store your yogurt, remember to allow it to soften a little before serving; you will get a much better flavor and a softer texture if you do this (15 to 20 minutes).

# Strawberry Yogurt

1½ cups puréed strawberries
(14 oz. fresh or frozen)
½ cup corn syrup
2 cups plain yogurt

**Yield:** About 1 quart

**Prep time:** 20 minutes

**Cook time:** None

1. Wash and remove green tops from strawberries, place in a blender or food processor, and purée.

2. Add corn syrup to strawberry purée and blend.

3. Place purée/corn syrup mixture and yogurt in a mixing bowl and, mix until smooth (no lumps).

4. Cool mixture to 40°F in your refrigerator.

5. Place the cold mixture into the ice cream freezer and freeze according to manufacturer's directions for making yogurt.

# Chocolate Yogurt

2¼ cups plain yogurt
1¾ cups chocolate syrup
½ cup table sugar
1 TB. crème de cocoa liqueur (optional but gives a great taste)

**Yield:** About 1 quart

**Prep time:** 15 minutes

**Cook time:** None

1. In a mixing bowl combine the yogurt, chocolate syrup, sugar, and crème de cocoa and mix until smooth (no lumps).

2. Cool mixture to 40°F in your refrigerator.

3. Place cold mixture into the ice cream freezer and freeze according to manufacturer's instructions for making yogurt.

# Vanilla Yogurt

3 cups plain yogurt

1 cup table sugar

2 TB. vanilla extract

| **Yield:** About 1 quart |
| --- |
| **Prep time:** 10 minutes |
| **Cook time:** None |

1. Mix together the yogurt, sugar, and vanilla extract until mixture is smooth (no lumps).

2. Cool mixture to 40°F in your refrigerator.

3. Place cold mixture into the ice cream freezer and freeze according to manufacturer's directions for making yogurt.

# Cranberry Yogurt

1 can cranberry sauce (whole or jelled)

2½ cups plain yogurt

½ cup table sugar

| **Yield:** About 1 quart |
| --- |
| **Prep time:** 10 minutes |
| **Cook time:** None |

1. In a mixing bowl combine the cranberries, yogurt, and sugar. Mix until smooth (no lumps).

2. Cool mixture to 40°F in your refrigerator.

3. Place the cold mixture into the ice cream freezer and freeze according to manufacturer's instructions for making yogurt.

# White Chocolate Coconut Yogurt

3 cups plain yogurt

½ cup corn syrup

3 bars white coconut chocolate

| **Yield:** About 1 quart |
| **Prep time:** 20 minutes |
| **Cook time:** 10 minutes |

1. In a mixing bowl combine plain yogurt and corn syrup. Set aside.

2. In a double boiler over low heat, melt white chocolate bars. Remove from heat.

3. Slowly add small amount of yogurt mixture to hot white chocolate and stir rapidly to incorporate. Do this several times to slowly cool the white chocolate mixture.

4. Add remaining hot white chocolate to yogurt mixture and blend well (no lumps).

5. Cool mixture to 40°F in your refrigerator.

6. Place the cold mixture into the ice cream freezer and freeze according to manufacturer's instructions for making yogurt.

# Banana Yogurt

5 large ripe bananas, puréed

½ cup sweetened condensed milk

2 cups plain yogurt

1 cup whole milk

1 TB. unflavored gelatin (1 oz.)

¼ cup water

| **Yield:** About 1 quart |
| --- |
| **Prep time:** 15 minutes |
| **Cook time:** 5 minutes |

1. Sprinkle gelatin over the water and allow to sit until completely dehydrated (10 to 15 minutes).

2. In a blender purée bananas and condensed milk.

3. In a mixing bowl combine banana mixture with yogurt and milk. Mix well (no lumps).

4. When gelatin has dehydrated, add to yogurt mixture and mix well (no lumps).

5. Cool mixture to 40°F in your refrigerator.

6. Place cold mixture into the ice cream freezer and freeze according to manufacturer's instructions for making yogurt.

# Cantaloupe Yogurt

1 large cantaloupe (2 cups puréed)

¾ cup table sugar

2 cups plain yogurt

| **Yield:** About 1 quart |
| --- |
| **Prep time:** 20 minutes |
| **Cook time:** None |

1. Peel cantaloupe and place pulp in a blender or food processor with sugar. Blend until smooth.

2. In a mixing bowl combine plain yogurt, cantaloupe, and sugar, mix until sugar is dissolved (no lumps).

3. Cool mixture to 40°F in your refrigerator.

4. Place cold mixture into the ice cream freezer and freeze according to manufacturer's instructions for making yogurt.

# Mocha Yogurt

1 TB. unflavored gelatin (1 oz.)

¼ cup water

¾ cup whole milk

¾ cup table sugar

¼ cup corn syrup

1 TB. instant coffee

¾ cup chocolate syrup

2 cups plain yogurt

**Yield:** About 1 quart

**Prep time:** 20 minutes

**Cook time:** 10 minutes

1. Dissolve gelatin in water and allow to sit until completely hydrated (10 to 15 minuets).

2. In a heavy saucepan scald milk while stirring constantly. Remove from heat and add sugar stirring until dissolved.

3. Add coffee, gelatin, and chocolate syrup, stirring until coffee and gelatin are combined. Allow to cool in the refrigerator.

4. In a mixing bowl combine yogurt and cool milk mixture. Mix well (no lumps).

5. Cool mixture to 40°F in your refrigerator.

6. Place cold mixture into the ice cream freezer and freeze according to manufacturer's instructions for making yogurt.

# Maple Yogurt

2½ cups plain yogurt
¾ cup pure maple syrup
¾ cup light cream

**Yield:** About 1 quart

**Prep time:** 15 minutes

**Cook time:** None

1. In a mixing bowl combine yogurt, maple syrup, and light cream. Mix well (no lumps).

2. Cool mixture to 40°F in your refrigerator.

3. Place cold mixture into the ice cream freezer and freeze according to manufacturer's instructions for making yogurt.

### Cool Tips

None of the yogurt recipes are set in stone; add or remove ingredients to your taste but remember to keep the volume. These recipes can be doubled or tripled depending on your need.

# Orange Marmalade Yogurt

2½ cups plain yogurt
1 (12-oz.) jar orange marmalade
¾ cup sweetened condensed milk
1 cup half-and-half

**Yield:** About 1 quart

**Prep time:** 15 minutes

**Cook time:** None

1. In a mixing bowl combine yogurt, orange marmalade, condensed milk, and half-and-half. Mix well (no lumps).

2. Cool mixture to 40°F in your refrigerator.

3. Place cold mixture into the ice cream freezer and freeze according to manufacturer's instructions for making yogurt.

# Peach Yogurt

1 TB. unflavored gelatin (1 oz.)

¼ cup water

3 ripe peaches (1 cup puréed)

½ cup table sugar

½ cup whole milk

2 cups plain yogurt

| **Yield:** About 1 quart |
| --- |
| **Prep time:** 25 minutes |
| **Cook time:** 15 minutes |

1. Sprinkle gelatin over the water and allow to sit until completely dehydrated (10 to 15 minutes).

2. Wash and pit peaches. Do not peel.

3. In a blender purée peaches with sugar and milk until smooth.

4. In a mixing bowl combine the peach purée mixture, gelatin, and yogurt. Mix until well blended (no lumps).

5. Cool mixture to 40°F in your refrigerator.

6. Place cold mixture into the ice cream freezer and freeze according to manufacturer's instructions for making yogurt.

# Brown Sugar Yogurt

2¼ cups plain yogurt

1¼ cups unpacked light brown sugar

½ cup corn syrup

| **Yield:** About 1 quart |
| **Prep time:** 15 minutes |
| **Cook time:** None |

1. In a blender, combine yogurt, brown sugar, and corn syrup. Blend ingredients together until brown sugar is totally incorporated.

2. Cool mixture to 40°F in your refrigerator. (At this point you may want to mix ingredients again to make sure brown sugar is totally dissolved.)

3. Place cold into the ice cream freezer and freeze according to manufacturer's instructions for making yogurt.

# Apricot Yogurt

5–6 ripe apricots (1 cup puréed)

½ cup table sugar

½ cup sweetened condensed milk

2 cups plain yogurt

| **Yield:** About 1 quart |
| **Prep time:** 20 minutes |
| **Cook time:** None |

1. Wash and pit apricots. Do not peel.

2. In a blender purée the apricots with sugar and condensed milk until smooth.

3. In a mixing bowl combine yogurt and apricot purée mixture. Mix well (no lumps).

4. Cool mixture to 40°F in your refrigerator.

5. Place cold mixture into the ice cream freezer and freeze according to manufacturer's instructions for making yogurt.

# Coffee Yogurt

1½ cups whole milk

1 TB. unflavored gelatin (1 oz.)

2 TB. instant coffee

¾ cup table sugar

2½ cups plain yogurt

**Yield:** About 1 quart

**Prep time:** 20 minutes

**Cook time:** 10 minutes

1. Sprinkle gelatin over ½ cup of milk and allow to sit until completely dehydrated (10 to 15 minutes).

2. Over low heat mix 1 cup milk, sugar, and instant coffee. Heat until coffee and sugar are dissolved. Remove from heat, add gelatin mixture, and mix until incorporated.

3. Allow mixture to cool in the refrigerator.

4. In a mixing bowl combine cool coffee mixture and yogurt. Mix well (no lumps).

5. Cool mixture to 40°F in your refrigerator.

6. Place cold mixture into the ice cream freezer and freeze according to manufacturer's instructions for making yogurt.

# Chapter 12

# Gelato

## In This Chapter

- ☺ What is gelato?
- ☺ Gelato ingredients

*Gelato* is the Italian word for ice cream. *Gelo* in Italian means "cold" and *Gielato* means "frost."

"*Gelaterias,*" which is the Italian name used for ice cream and frozen dessert shops, originally sold a product more like sorbet. But through the years sorbet evolved as a creamier, more dense product, which we now call "gelato."

Gelato is different from what we think of as ice cream, mainly because it tends to have a very intense flavor and is eaten in a semi-frozen state. As with frozen yogurt, there are no government standards or specific definitions for its content. So there are a wide variety of gelato recipes. The difference between American gelatos, which taste more like ice cream, and the Italian style is often very noticeable in texture and consistency.

Normally, gelato is made with less cream and more milk than most ice creams, but they usually include more eggs, which are used as stabilizers. They also typically require more sugar as a

### Avoid a Meltdown

Because it contains less butterfat and sweeteners (stabilizers), gelato is much better served on the same day that it is made and at a softer texture. It actually tastes better served at a higher temperature. If frozen in a deep freezer, the iciness is more prevalent due to the absence of the butterfat.

sweetener. The richness comes from the eggs along with less air whipped in ("overrun") than the American ice creams. Because it is lower in butterfat, which requires more eggs, flavoring, and less whipping to give it density.

Generally, gelato recipes use approximately 1 to 2 cups of water, 1 cup of sugar, 2 cups of fresh fruit or other ingredients, 3 cups of milk, and 5 to 25 grams of stabilizer (gelatin). Gelato is typically made with fruit, chocolate, nuts, small candies, or cookies. Nut flavors like pistachio and hazelnut are especially popular. When displayed properly in trays in a gelato cabinet or display case, it is very colorful and attractive, with lots of eye appeal.

For gelato flavors, as with frozen yogurts, I tried to pick flavors and recipes that are popular from that part of the industry and that are adaptable for this special category of frozen desserts.

# Zabaglione Gelato

8 egg yolks

¾ cup table sugar

4 cups whole milk

1 tsp. vanilla extract

1 cup dry Marsala wine

| **Yield:** About 2 quarts |
| --- |
| **Prep time:** 40 minutes |
| **Cook time:** 20 minutes |

1. Beat egg yolks and sugar together until they are light and fluffy.

2. In a heavy saucepan over medium heat, combine egg mixture and milk. Cook until temperature reaches 160°F (coats back of spoon). Remove from heat and place in an ice bath until cold.

3. When mixture is cool, place in a mixing bowl and add the vanilla extract and Marsala wine. Mix well.

4. Cool mixture to 40°F in your refrigerator.

5. Place cold mixture into the ice cream freezer and freeze according to manufacturer's instructions for making ice cream.

**Variation:**

Substitute champagne or sweet sherry for the Marsala wine.

**Tasty Terms**

*Zabaglione* translates to "great foam."

# Banana Gelato

8 egg yolks

¾ cup table sugar

4 cups whole milk

6 ripe medium bananas

1 TB. banana liqueur (optional)

**Yield:** About 2 quarts

**Prep time:** 40 minutes

**Cook time:** 10 minutes

1. Beat egg yolks and sugar together until light and fluffy.

2. In the top of a double boiler over medium heat, combine the sugar mixture with 3 cups milk and cook until temperature reaches 160°F (coats back of spoon). Remove from heat and place in an ice bath until cold.

3. Peel and purée bananas in a blender or food processor.

4. When egg mixture is cold, place in a mixing bowl and add remaining milk and banana liqueur. Mix well.

5. Cool mixture to 40°F in your refrigerator.

6. Place cold mixture into the ice cream freezer and freeze according to manufacturer's instructions for making ice cream.

# Vanilla Gelato

9 egg yolks

¾ cup table sugar

1 vanilla bean

5 cups whole milk

| **Yield:** About 2 quarts |
| --- |
| **Prep time:** 40 minutes |
| **Cook time:** 20 minutes |

1. Beat egg yolks and sugar together until light and fluffy.

2. Cut vanilla bean in half; scrape out seeds on both sides and add them into the egg mixture. Cut up vanilla pod very finely and also add to the egg mixture.

3. In the top of a double boiler over medium heat, combine sugar mixture and 3 cups milk. Cook until temperature reaches 160°F (coats back of spoon). Remove from heat and place in an ice bath until cold.

4. When cold, strain the egg mixture through a sieve to remove the larger pieces of the vanilla bean.

5. Cool mixture to 40°F in your refrigerator.

6. Place cold mixture into the ice cream freezer and freeze according to manufacturer's instructions for making ice cream.

# Apricot Gelato

8 egg yolks

¾ cup of table sugar

5 cups whole milk

1 tsp. lemon juice

24 oz. apricot preserves

1 TB. apricot liqueur (optional)

**Yield:** About 2 quarts

**Prep time:** 40 minutes

**Cook time:** 20 minutes

1. Beat egg yolks and sugar together until light and fluffy.

2. In the top of a double boiler over medium heat, combine the egg mixture with 3 cups milk and cook until temperature reaches 160°F (coats back of spoon). Remove from heat and place in an ice bath until cold.

3. Melt apricot preserves in a saucepan over low heat. Remove from heat and place melted apricots in a blender and purée for about 1 minute or until preserve is smooth. Allow to cool.

4. Add puréed apricots, remaining milk, lemon juice, and apricot liqueur to cold egg mixture and mix until blended.

5. Cool mixture to 40°F in your refrigerator.

6. Place cold mixture into the ice cream freezer and freeze according to manufacturer's instructions for making ice cream.

# Chocolate Gelato

6 egg yolks

1 cup table sugar

5 cups whole milk

6 oz. unsweetened baking chocolate (grated into small pieces)

1 TB. crème de cocoa liqueur (optional)

**Yield:** About 2 quarts

**Prep time:** 40 minutes

**Cook time:** 20 minutes

1. Beat egg yolks and sugar until light and fluffy.

2. In the top of a double boiler over medium heat, combine the egg mixture with 3 cups milk and cook until mixture reaches 160°F (coats back of spoon). Remove from heat and place in an ice bath until cold.

3. In the top of a double boiler over low heat, combine milk and grated chocolate, and heat until chocolate is completely melted. Remove from heat.

4. Place cold egg mixture into a mixing bowl and very slowly, a little at a time, pour in the chocolate mixture. Add remaining milk and crème de cocoa. Mix well.

5. Cool mixture to 40°F in your refrigerator.

6. Place cold mixture into the ice cream freezer and freeze according to manufacturer's instructions for making ice cream.

# Cheese Gelato

5 egg yolks

¾ cup table sugar

3 cups whole milk

17 oz. ricotta cheese

Zest from 1 lemon

1½ tsp. vanilla extract

**Yield:** About 2 quarts

**Prep time:** 20 minutes

**Cook time:** 10 minutes

1. Beat egg yolks and sugar until light and fluffy.

2. In the top of a double boiler over medium heat, combine the egg mixture and milk, cook until temperature reaches 160°F (coats back of spoon). Remove from heat and place in an ice bath until cold.

3. In a food processor or blender purée the ricotta, lemon zest, and vanilla until smooth.

4. Add cheese mixture to cold egg mixture and mix until well blended.

5. Cool mixture to 40°F in your refrigerator.

6. Place cold mixture into the ice cream freezer and freeze according to manufacturer's instructions for making ice cream.

# Coffee Gelato

7 egg yolks

1 cup table sugar

5 cups whole milk

2 TB. instant coffee (or to taste)

1 TB. vanilla extract

1 TB. Kahlua liqueur (optional)

| |
|---|
| **Yield:** About 2 quarts |
| **Prep time:** 30 minutes |
| **Cook time:** 10 minutes |

1. Beat egg yolks and sugar until light and fluffy.

2. In the top of a double boiler over medium heat, cook egg mixture with 3 cups milk until the temperature reaches 160°F (coats back of spoon). Remove from heat and place in an ice bath until cold.

3. In a sauce pan, over low heat combine 2 cups milk with the instant coffee and heat just enough to dissolve the coffee. Remove from heat.

4. Place cold egg mixture into a mixing bowl and combine the coffee mixture, vanilla extract, and Kahlua liqueur. Mix well.

5. Cool mixture to 40°F in your refrigerator.

6. Place cold mixture into the ice cream freezer and freeze according to manufacturer's instructions for making ice cream.

**Part 4**

# Toppings

Even the best ice cream flavors can sometimes use that little something extra, so I'll spend the next few chapters discussing ways to give your dessert the perfect finishing touch. I'll start with the old favorites: sauces made from hot fudge and butterscotch. Then I'll move on to fruit sauces, and from there I'll share recipes for more unusual toppings. Candies and nuts are very popular dessert toppings, so I'll spend some time discussing variations along those lines, too.

# Chapter 13

# The Classic Toppers

## In This Chapter

- ◌ Why toppings can be fun
- ◌ Toppings that are "hot" with consumers
- ◌ New takes on classic hot fudge

Sure, your ice cream may be wonderful as is, all by itself. But even the best flavors can get boring after a while. Or maybe you're just in the mood for something different. This is where toppings come in. They can give your ice cream that extra special touch. Thinking up and experimenting with toppings, syrups, and sauces for your dessert can be just as much fun as the ice cream they cover. Yes, here too, the choices seem endless. And although I have included many interesting recipes to prepare, you may find, in your kitchen, other ingredients that can be used as a topping. An example of that might be maple syrup or peanut butter.

Making toppings isn't that difficult, but if you wish to save some time, numerous toppings and sauces are sold in your local grocery stores. I sell my homemade topping and sauce in quarts and pints to my customers, and I'm sure that your local ice cream shop would do the same. Just ask!

# The Most Popular Toppings

At my ice cream shop, the homemade chocolate hot fudge outsells all other toppings 20 to 1, with butterscotch running a distant second. In fact, the heated toppings are 70 to 80 percent of the public's choice. The figures would probably be similar at many other shops across the country. Bottom line is, people really like heated toppings on their ice cream.

Since the hot sauces seem to be among the most popular toppings, I thought I'd start with those.

**Cool Tips**

I have often used liqueurs as a topping at home, especially on vanilla ice cream, but they can also be used as "back-up" flavors to give a boost to other homemade toppings—for example, crème de cocoa added to your hot fudge.

# Hot Fudge Sauce

¼ cup butter (unsalted)

2 oz. unsweetened baking chocolate

¾ cup table sugar

2 TB. unsweetened cocoa powder

½ cup whipping cream

1 tsp. vanilla extract

| | |
|---|---|
| **Yield:** About 1½ cups | |
| **Prep time:** 35 minutes | |
| **Cook time:** 20 minutes | |

1. In a double boiler over low heat, melt unsweetened chocolate with butter, stirring occasionally.

2. In a mixing bowl mix together cocoa and sugar. Stir in whipping cream and mix well.

3. Add cocoa/sugar mixture to melted chocolate in the top of a double boiler. Cook over low heat until cocoa and sugar are dissolved. Remove from heat and cool slightly.

4. After chocolate has cooled for about 5 minutes, whisk in vanilla.

5. Can be served hot or cold and keeps well in the refrigerator.

# Chocolate Fudge Sauce Topping

5 oz. semisweet baking chocolate

3 oz. unsweetened baking chocolate

4 TB. unsalted butter

½ cup heavy cream

½ cup table sugar

⅓ cup corn syrup

1 tsp. vanilla extract

**Yield:** About 2 cups

**Prep time:** 25 minutes

**Cook time:** 15 minutes

1. In a double boiler over low heat, melt semisweet and unsweetened chocolate and butter.

2. Heat heavy cream, corn syrup, and sugar in a saucepan until sugar is dissolved.

3. Pour warm cream mixture and vanilla into melted chocolate and mix to incorporate. Remove from heat.

4. Can be served hot or cold and keeps well in the refrigerator.

 **Cool Tips**

Hot fudge goes well with many base flavors besides vanilla. Be creative. How about trying it with peppermint, mint chip, or coconut ice cream?

# Quick Hot Fudge

1 cup table sugar

½ cup unsweetened cocoa powder

1 cup light corn syrup

½ cup light cream

3 TB. unsalted butter

¾ tsp. vanilla extract

**Yield:** About 2 cups

**Prep time:** 15 minutes

**Cook time:** 15 minutes

1. In a mixing bowl combine sugar and cocoa. Mix well.

2. In a heavy saucepan combine cocoa mixture, corn syrup, and light cream. Over medium heat cook until cocoa mixture is dissolved.

3. Lower heat and add butter. Continue cooking until butter is melted. Remove from heat and cool slightly.

4. When mixture is slightly cooled, whisk in vanilla extract.

5. Can be served hot or cold and keeps well in the refrigerator.

**Variations:**

Try putting walnuts in the syrup, or adding butterscotch with mini marshmallows (this is called a "Midwesterner").

By adding pineapple, you get what was known as a "Hoboken" in the 1940s and 1950s.

Try adding raspberries or strawberries for a sweet, fruity flair. Or add malt powder, and you've got yourself a "Dusty Road."

If you use chocolate ice cream and add nuts and black cherries, you can enjoy a "Black Forest."

A final idea is to use cake crumbs or pieces of brownies or graham crackers under the ice cream or above the hot fudge.

### Avoid a Meltdown

Do not add vanilla extract or liqueurs to a very hot mixture, because the alcohol will quickly evaporate and lose some of its flavoring abilities.

## Butterscotch Sauce

1½ cups packed light brown sugar

½ cup light corn syrup

⅓ cup butter

⅔ cup heavy cream

> **Yield:** About 2 cups
>
> **Prep time:** 20 minutes
>
> **Cook time:** 15 minutes

1. In a heavy saucepan combine butter, corn syrup, and brown sugar and cook over medium heat until mixture thickens. Stir constantly. Remove from heat.

2. When mixture has cooled for a few minutes, add cream and mix until smooth.

3. Can be served hot or cold and keeps well in the refrigerator.

## Caramel Sauce

1½ cups sugar

¾ cup boiling water

¼ cup heavy cream

3 TB. butter

> **Yield:** About 1½ cups
>
> **Prep time:** 20 minutes
>
> **Cook time:** 10 minutes

1. In a nonstick pan cook sugar over low heat, stirring often, until sugar melts and turns a golden brown. Remove from heat.

2. Add boiling water to cooked sugar and mix to combine. Return to heat and cook until mixture starts to thicken. Remove from heat. Cool slightly.

3. Add heavy cream and butter. Mix well.

4. Can be served hot or cold and keeps well in the refrigerator.

# Quick Caramel Sauce

¾ lb. caramel candies
¾ cup light cream

| **Yield:** About 2 cups |
| --- |
| **Prep time:** 15 minutes |
| **Cook time:** 10 minutes |

1. In a double boiler over low heat, place unwrapped candies and melt.

2. Remove from heat and slowly pour in light cream. If needed, return mixture to the heat to incorporate.

3. Can be served hot or cold and keeps well in the refrigerator.

# Chapter 14

# Fruit-Based Sauces

## In This Chapter

- ☺ The most common fruit sauces
- ☺ Tips for getting the best taste

Strawberry, blueberry, pineapple, and raspberry are probably among the most popular fruit sauces for ice cream. But they are by no means the only choices. There's also cranberry, banana, cherry, apricot, and many other options.

For an easy and quick way to make fruit sauces or toppings I have used jams, jellies, and preserves. You will have to thin these by using simple syrup (recipe in Chapter 9) or corn syrup. Another nice way to serve these toppings and sauces is to heat them.

I think the process of making fruit sauces is pretty straightforward. I've tried to make the recipes as basic and easy to understand as possible. So you should do fine, even if you've never made a fruit sauce before. But there are easy ways to increase your odds of success. Obviously, you should try to find fruit that is as fresh as possible.

# Orange Sauce

¾ cup table sugar

1 cup fresh orange juice

2 TB. Grand Marnier liqueur

**Yield:** About 1¼ cups

**Prep time:** 20 minutes

**Cook time:** 10 minutes

1. In a heavy saucepan boil sugar and orange juice for about 3 minutes or until it becomes syrupy.

2. Remove from heat, cool for 2 minutes and stir in Grand Marnier.

3. Can be served hot or cold. Will keep well in the refrigerator.

# Raspberry Sauce

24 oz. fresh raspberries

½ cup table sugar

2 TB. Kirsch liqueur (optional)

**Yield:** About 2 cups

**Prep time:** 20 minutes

**Cook time:** None

1. In a blender combine raspberries, sugar, and Kirsch, and purée.

2. Strain mixture through a sieve to remove raspberry seeds.

3. Serve cold.

# Lemon Sauce

⅓ cup table sugar

1 TB. cornstarch

⅛ tsp. of salt

1 cup hot water

¼ cup lemon juice

1 TB. butter

**Yield:** About 1½ cups

**Prep time:** 20 minutes

**Cook time:** 10 minutes

1. In a heavy saucepan over medium heat, combine sugar, cornstarch, salt, and hot water.

2. Cook until mixture is thick and clear, stirring constantly. Remove from heat.

3. Stir in lemon juice and butter.

4. Best served warm.

# Apricot Sauce

5–6 ripe apricots

½ cup table sugar

1 tsp. cornstarch

½ cup water

**Yield:** About 2 cups

**Prep time:** 30 minutes

**Cook time:** 10 minutes

1. Wash and pit apricots. Do not peel.

2. Place apricots and sugar in a blender or food processor and purée. At this time, add sugar to taste.

3. In a heavy saucepan over medium heat, cook cornstarch and water until thick and clear. Remove from heat.

4. In a mixing bowl combine the apricot purée with cornstarch mixture. Taste. If not sweet enough add more sugar.

5. Serve warm.

# Pineapple Topping

½ cup table sugar

1 TB. cornstarch

1 (20-oz.) can crushed pineapple

1½ TB. butter

¼ cup water

**Yield:** About 3 cups

**Prep time:** 20 minutes

**Cook time:** 10 minutes

1. In a heavy saucepan over medium heat, combine sugar and cornstarch. Add crushed pineapple with juice, butter, and water.

2. Bring mixture to a boil, stirring constantly.

3. Lower heat to a simmer and continue cooking for three minutes, continuing to stir.

4. Taste. If not sweet enough, add more sugar and stir until dissolved.

5. Serve warm or cold.

# Strawberry Sauce

1 qt. fresh or frozen strawberries, whole

½ cup water

½ cup light corn syrup

**Yield:** About 2 cups

**Prep time:** 20 minutes

**Cook time:** 10 minutes

1. Wash and remove green from fresh strawberries.

2. In a heavy saucepan combine whole strawberries, water, and corn syrup. Cook over low heat until strawberries are softened.

3. Remove from heat and partially mash strawberries, leaving some large chunks.

4. Serve cold.

# Cherry Topping

1 (16-oz.) jar maraschino
cherries

¼ cup water

1 TB. cornstarch

**Yield:** About 1½ cups

**Prep time:** 20 minutes

**Cook time:** 10 minutes

1. Drain juice from cherries, enough for ¾ cup juice.

2. Take half of cherries from the jar and purée in a blender or food processor. Set aside.

3. Take the other half of cherries and chop into medium to large pieces. Set aside.

4. In a heavy saucepan over medium heat, combine cherry juice, water, and cornstarch. Heat until mixture thickens.

5. Remove mixture from heat and add cherry purée. Return mixture to heat and bring to a boil again.

6. Remove from heat and stir in chopped cherries.

7. Can be served warm or cold.

 **Cool Tips**

Use your own judgment and taste preferences to determine how small to cut up the fruit pieces for your sauce. You may even decide to purée them.

 **The Real Scoop**

To get a great flavor from your fruits, try letting them sit overnight with sugar sprinkled on top. When mixed together the next day, the fruit tends to make its own syrup.

# Chapter 15

# Other Sauces

## In This Chapter

- Additional sauce ideas
- What goes into whipped toppings?
- Other topping ideas

I've covered the classic toppings, and the other category of common sauces—those that are fruit based. But you can still find many other topping ideas that can add a fun twist to your favorite ice cream.

In this chapter, I'll share ideas for a diverse range of sauce and topping ideas, from a wine sauce to one featuring walnuts in syrup. I'll also discuss candy, nuts, and other mix-ins.

Again, you can give these sauces your own personal flair in countless ways. Try using ice cream in a flavor other than vanilla, or add in some candies or other extras.

## Whipped Toppings

Most people like to top off their desserts with whipped cream, either homemade or store bought. It's such an easy topping to make that you really don't even need a recipe. If you take heavy cream and beat it, Voilà! You have whipped cream. However, people tend to like their toppings to be a little sweeter, so they often add sugar and/or vanilla. In this chapter, I will give you one recipe and then lots of ways to change the flavor and color

# Other Mix-Ins

Here is a list of add-ons that you can pour on top of sauces, or use as toppings all on their own:

- ○ Nuts: any kind of nut you can imagine, chopped or whole
- ○ Fruits: any fruit you like, cut into small pieces
- ○ Candies/candy bars: whatever you like, broken into small pieces
- ○ Baked goods: brownies, cookies, cakes, crackers broken into small pieces
- ○ Dried fruit: dates, raisins, cranberries, coconut flakes
- ○ Cereals: granola, honey nut, grape nut, or barely nut
- ○ Jams and jellies: any you can make or purchase in your grocery store (warmed)

# Claret Sauce

1 cup table sugar
½ cup water
2 TB. lemon juice
1 cup claret wine

**Yield:** About 1½ cups

**Prep time:** 20 minutes

**Cook time:** 10 minutes

1. Place water and sugar in a heavy saucepan, and boil for 5 minutes.

2. Remove from heat and add lemon juice and claret wine. Mix well.

3. Set mixture in an ice bath until cold.

4. This sauce is served cold.

# Marshmallow Sauce

1½ dozen large marshmallows
½ cup light cream
1 tsp. vanilla extract

**Yield:** About 1¼ cups

**Prep time:** 15 minutes

**Cook time:** 10 minutes

1. In the top of a double boiler over boiling water, heat marshmallows and cream until marshmallows are almost melted. Remove from heat and continue stirring until marshmallows are totally melted. Cool for several minutes.

2. Add vanilla and mix well.

3. Sauce can be served hot or cold.

# Ginger Sauce

1 cup table sugar

1 cup water

¾ crystallized ginger (cut into pieces)

**Yield:** About 1½ cups

**Prep time:** 10 minutes

**Cook time:** 6 minutes

1. In a heavy saucepan over high heat, boil sugar and water until it reaches a syrup consistency. Add ginger and cook for 1 minute.

2. Remove from heat.

3. I like to serve this sauce while it is still hot, but warm will do nicely. It will keep in your refrigerator in a covered jar and can be reheated.

# Maple Sauce

½ cup sugar

¼ cup corn syrup

¾ cup light cream

3 TB. butter

¾ cup real maple syrup

**Yield:** About 1½ cups

**Prep time:** 20 minutes

**Cook time:** 10 minutes

1. In a heavy saucepan over high heat, heat sugar, corn syrup, and cream until it reaches the soft boil stage (240°F). (One drop of liquid into cold water should form a soft ball on the bottom of the water container.)

2. Remove from heat and add butter and maple syrup, mixing until combined.

3. Can be used hot or cold, and can be kept in the refrigerator.

# Pecan Mocha Sauce

1 cup sugar
⅓ cup strong coffee
3 oz. semisweet chocolate
⅓ cup evaporated milk
¾ cup chopped pecans

**Yield:** About 1½ cups

**Prep time:** 20 minutes

**Cook time:** 10 minutes

1. In a heavy saucepan boil sugar and coffee until it reaches the soft ball stage (240°F). (One drop of liquid into cold water should form a soft ball on the bottom of the water container.)

2. Melt chocolate in the top of a double boiler over low heat, until smooth and creamy. Remove from heat.

3. Add chocolate to hot sugar/ coffee mixture and blend until smooth. (If mixture is lumpy, return to medium heat and stir until smooth.)

4. Add evaporated milk to chocolate/coffee mixture and blend until creamy. Add nuts and mix well.

5. Sauce can be served hot or cold. Mixture will not hold well in the refrigerator and the nuts tend to get soggy.

# Melba Sauce

2 cups raspberry purée (fresh or frozen)
½ cup table sugar
1 tsp. cornstarch

**Yield:** About 2 cups

**Prep time:** 15 minutes

**Cook time:** 5 minutes

1. In a blender purée the raspberries.

2. Place raspberry purée in a heavy saucepan. Add sugar and cornstarch. Cook over medium heat for approximately five minutes, stirring constantly. Mixture should be slightly thick.

3. Remove from heat and cool.

4. This sauce has more flavor when served cold. Can be kept in the refrigerator.

# Date Topping

10 oz. pitted dates

½ cup light corn syrup

**Yield:** About 2 cups

**Prep time:** 20 minutes

**Cook time:** 10 minutes

1. In a blender or food processor, purée pitted dates with corn syrup. Taste the purée, and add more corn syrup if needed.

2. Can be served warm or cold.

3. A 20-second zap in the microwave will warm mixture.

# Honey Topping

¼ cup light cream

1 TB. cornstarch

1½ cups honey

**Yield:** About 1½ cups

**Prep time:** 10 minutes

**Cook time:** 5 minutes

1. In a heavy saucepan over medium heat, combine cream and cornstarch. Stir constantly until cornstarch is dissolved.

2. Add honey to cream mixture and bring to a boil. Boil for 1 minute, stirring constantly.

3. Remove from heat.

4. Serve warm.

## Peanut Butter Brown Sugar Sauce

1 cup packed light brown sugar

1 tsp. cornstarch

⅛ tsp. salt

1 cup water

½ cup peanut butter (smooth or chunky)

1 tsp. vanilla extract (optional)

**Yield:** About 2 cups

**Prep time:** 20 minutes

**Cook time:** 10 minutes

1. In a heavy saucepan combine sugar, cornstarch, and salt. Add water and cook over medium heat until mixture comes to a boil. Remove from heat.

2. Stir in peanut butter until smooth. (You may have to return mixture to the stove to help combine the peanut butter.)

3. Remove from heat and add optional vanilla.

4. Can be served hot or cold.

## Walnuts in Syrup

1 cup table sugar

1 cup light corn syrup

¼ cup water

¼ cup pure maple syrup

2 cups chopped walnuts

**Yield:** About 2 cups

**Prep time:** 20 minutes

**Cook time:** 10 minutes

1. In a heavy saucepan combine sugar, corn syrup, water, and maple syrup. Over medium heat stir until sugar is dissolved. Remove from heat.

2. Add walnuts to mixture and allow to cool.

3. Serve at room temperature.

# Whipped Cream Topping

2 cups whipped cream, very
cold

¼ cup powdered sugar or table
sugar

1 tsp. vanilla extract

| **Yield:** About 2 cups |
| --- |
| **Prep time:** 10 minutes |
| **Cook time:** None |

1. In a chilled mixing bowl combine whipping cream, sugar, and
vanilla.

2. Using an electric mixer on
medium-high speed, whip mixture until soft peaks form.

3. Can be stored in the refrigerator
for up to three hours. (You may
have to rewhip.)

4. To make flavored whipped
creams, replace vanilla extract
with another flavored extract
or liqueur. Here are some possi-
bilities:

> Peppermint extract
> Maple extract
> Coffee extract
> Almond extract
> Lemon extract
> Coffee brandy
> Peach brandy
> Sambuca liqueur

I have used all of these flavors,
and before long I will probably
find new flavors to taste.

### The Real Scoop

Using food coloring in whipped cream is great for the holidays. Make
a batch, divide it in half, and use red and green food coloring for topping Christmas desserts. Or how about just green for St. Patrick's Day?
Be creative!

# Part 5

# Sundaes, Cones, and More

Now that you've become a wizard with the ice cream maker, I think it's time to celebrate. In these next few chapters, I'll help you do just that. By now, you know how to make ice cream in just about any flavor imaginable. In these next few chapters, I'll show you how to use that ice cream as the foundation for some excellent desserts. First, I'll cover the classic desserts like hot fudge sundaes and banana splits. Then, to celebrate your ice cream skills, I'll help you whip together some great party treats. Finally, for occasions when any boring cone or bowl just won't do, I'll show you how to make a delicious waffle cone.

# Chapter 16

# Classic Ice Cream Desserts

## In This Chapter

- ○ How the sundae got its name
- ○ Perfect parfaits
- ○ The makings of a great banana split
- ○ Ice Cream Sandwiches

In this chapter, I'll discuss some of the most common classic ice cream desserts: sundaes, banana splits, ice cream sandwiches, and parfaits. I'll also share ideas for making your own classic treat.

## The Sundae

Probably the most popular classic ice cream dessert is the sundae. If you're wondering how the sundae got its name, well, there are several different stories among ice cream folklore.

Some people believe the name got started because this dessert was special and expensive to serve, so it was served only on Sundays or on special occasions. However, most people believe that this dessert dish originated in the state of Massachusetts—or perhaps Illinois or Wisconsin—during the era when strict laws

> **Cool Tips**
>
> When you build a sundae, put a little sauce in the bottom of the glass or dish before adding the ice cream. This is part presentation and partly to save a taste until the last spoonful.

prohibited the sale of carbonated soft drinks from being served on Sunday.

An enterprising "soda jerk" is said to have omitted the carbonation from the ice cream soda and just placed syrup on the ice cream, and the name "sundae" stuck. Today, sundaes of all types, including banana splits, make up 60 to 75 percent of all fountain service.

Becoming a true master of the ice cream sundae takes time and practice. Some people even get a special education on the topic. Early on, there were sundae schools run by organizations like the International Association of Ice Cream Manufacturers. Yes, like ice cream sodas, making sundaes is an art form, not only because of the long list of combinations, but also the various dishes, goblets, glasses, bowls, and other items in which they are served.

Some fountain entrepreneurs stress that there must be a balance between the topping and the ice cream, so that when completed it con-

> **The Real Scoop**
>
> Sundaes were also called "College Ices" in the 1900s.

tains an equal amount of ice cream and topping. But an experienced sundae eater can usually handle that assignment very well by him- or herself.

In Chapter 13, I included several recipes for hot fudge toppings. By adding those to ice cream, you've got your basic hot fudge sundae. But there are many ways to put a new twist on this classic dessert favorite. Here are some variations on the basic hot fudge sundae:

- **Tin Roof.** Mix Spanish peanuts in the hot fudge.
- **Bull Moose.** Mix mini marshmallows with hot fudge and pour over ice cream, and add two tall cookies for the moose horns.
- **Crispy Fudge.** Mix hot fudge with any crispy or crunchy cereal.
- **Mud Pie.** Crush chocolate-cream-filled cookies into the hot fudge.
- **Snowball.** Roll small, round scoops of vanilla ice cream in chocolate syrup and coconut flakes.

- **Turtle.** Place half hot fudge and half caramel topping on either side of your favorite ice cream flavor.

- **Candy Store.** Mix any type of candy bar (crushed) with the hot fudge.

- **Espresso.** Mix coffee ice cream with hot fudge and crumbled oatmeal cookies.

- **Peanut Butter Cup.** Hot fudge with peanut butter topping and/or peanut butter and chocolate candy bars cut up small and mixed together.

- **Raisin in the Sun.** Add chopped raisins to the hot fudge and serve over orange sherbet.

- **Fudgiana.** Cut bananas into round slices and mix with hot fudge.

- **Sherbet Ambrosia.** Put orange and banana slices on orange sherbet with shredded coconut.

- **Christmas Sundae.** Pour cranberry or cranberry-orange sauce on vanilla ice cream.

- **Southern Belle Sundae.** Add pineapple, marshmallow sauce, and cherries to orange or lemon sherbet.

- **New England Cranberry Maple Walnut Sundae.** Mix maple syrup with dried cranberries.

- **Peanut Brittle Sundae.** Crush peanut brittle and sprinkle over butterscotch topping.

- **Snowdrops Sundae.** Mix marshmallow with fresh orange slices.

- **Beehive Sundae.** Pour honey sauce with salted almonds over the top of your favorite ice cream, and top with whipped cream.

- **Cherry Jubilee Sundae.** Mix warm cherry sauce with whole cherries, pour over ice cream, and add whipped cream.

- **Chopped Suey Sundae.** Mix a layer of crushed pineapple with the same amount of chopped candied cherries or chopped dates in the bottom of a sundae dish, and scoop pistachio ice cream over it, and add a topper of whipped cream.

- **Pecan Maple Sundae.** Pour maple syrup over a scoop of vanilla ice cream, cover with chopped pecans, sprinkle a little cinnamon over the top, and add whipped cream.

- **Crème de Menthe Sundae.** Pour crème de menthe over the top of vanilla ice cream, and add whipped cream.

○ **Orange Honey Sundae.** Pour apricot sauce and honey sauce over the top of vanilla and orange ice cream (or sherbet), and add whipped cream.

For parties, you can create extra large sundaes with hot fudge and any other topping to make your own sundae name such as "Pike's Peak" or "Mt. St. Helen's." Some other old-time sundae names are Knicker Bocker, Lone Star, Peg o' My Heart, Sweetheart, Blossom, Midnight Sun, Lady Mary, Roof Garden, September Moon, Hobble, Goo-Goo, and Cabaret.

# Parfaits

One of the most decorative ice cream desserts is the *parfait*. In French it means "perfect," and that's a fitting description. They can truly appear perfect with colorful layers of toppings, sauces, fruits, and/or liquors. The traditional parfait is made in a tall glass (somewhat like a pilsner) with up to three scoops of ice cream, and sauce in between each scoop. You will feel like an artist as you decide what colors and flavors to use.

Without a doubt, some of the most popular parfaits include fresh or frozen fruits. Suppose you are planning your Fourth of July party, and you have decided you want to serve a special dessert. Why not celebrate with a parfait of vanilla, strawberry, and blueberry ice cream, with sauces that complement the flavors? To complete the parfait, top it off with red, white, and blue whipped cream and a cherry.

**Cool Tips**

This chapter contains just a few samples of parfaits. You can use your own imagination and tastes to think of lots more. Even though I have given you ice cream and sauces, don't forget that you can add anything in between the layers. Candies, cookie, brownies, or granola are some favorites among my family. Just don't stray too much or you will be making sundaes.

# Banana Split

The ever-popular banana split is at least 100 years old. Like a lot of ice cream history, there are many claims as to its origins. It certainly has been a distinct favorite at ice cream shops for years. It takes a bit of preparation time, but the appeal of the split—sometimes called "banana royal"—lies in the combination of several flavors of ice cream and the variety of toppings, which blend well with ice cream, producing tremendous eye appeal. In fact, at my shop Four Seas Ice Cream, if they sell one or two at the tables or fountain, they usually get several more requests, once folks see the first one.

It varies in different parts of the country, but there is a basic or standard formulation that I will chart out, although your combinations once again are endless. If you don't like all flavors and mixtures running together, you can choose to section off each small sundae in a two- or three-section dish.

### The Real Scoop

According to one claim of its origin, the banana split was created in 1904 in a small town in Pennsylvania called Latrobe, and recently they had a celebration honoring its hundredth birthday. In fact, there is an interesting book, recently published, to commemorate the occasion and to exalt the virtues of the ice cream standard bearer. An apprentice pharmacist, named David Stricker, concocted the new sundae at Tassel's Pharmacy and it took off from there.

Original soda jerks felt that there was a correct position for the banana in a banana split dish. They wanted the seeds exposed to whet the customers appetite. Those same soda jerks had their own language when it came to ordering a banana split. They would shout "Split one!" or "Grab a house boat!"

The standard banana split today is still a banana, split down the middle, with a scoop of chocolate ice cream topped with hot fudge or chocolate sauce, a scoop of vanilla ice cream topped with pineapple sauce, and strawberry ice cream with strawberry sauce on top, plus a dollop of whipped cream on top of each sauce, a sprinkle of nuts, and don't forget the cherries. Yes, there are reportedly 150 or more versions of the split, with names like "Rocket Ship" and "Monkey's Heaven" and with bananas set vertically as well as horizontally; but the old standard in a true banana split dish will always be in demand.

# Ice Cream Sandwiches

Ice cream sandwiches have been around for at least 100 years. The tiny single serving "pie," wrapped and purchased at local grocery stores or from the neighborhood ice cream vendor truck, has a special place in people's memories of more youthful times. Today, with so many different cookies—whether store bought or homemade—and with ice cream that can be taken right from your deep freezer, it is easy to make them at home.

> **Avoid a Meltdown**
>
> I suggest you use hard cookies, as they will not break as easily. Another thing that I've found helpful is to make the cookies the day before making the ice cream sandwiches, allowing them time to sit out and harden a bit.

Don't limit yourself to just cookie ice cream sandwiches, when you can make brownie ice cream sandwiches. Ask any child—I bet they can come up with something special.

This chapter gives you a few recipes for making these delicious treats, but it won't take you long to come up with a few on your own.

# Maple Syrup Parfait

3 (2-oz.) scoops vanilla ice cream

3 TB. whipped cream

6 TB. maple syrup

| **Yield:** 1 parfait |
| --- |
| **Prep time:** 3 minutes |
| **Cook time:** None |

1. In a tall, slim glass place 1–2 oz. scoop vanilla ice cream, 1 table-spoon whipped cream, and 2 tablespoons maple syrup.

2. Repeat this process two more times.

3. Keep in the freezer until just before serving.

# Chocolate Parfait

3 (2-oz.) scoops chocolate ice cream

6 TB. chocolate sauce (cold)

| **Yield:** 1 parfait |
| --- |
| **Prep time:** 3 minutes |
| **Cook time:** None |

1. In a tall glass place 1–2 oz. scoop chocolate ice cream, and pour 2 tablespoons chocolate sauce over ice cream.

2. Repeat this process two more times.

3. Keep in the freezer until just before serving. Top with whipped cream and sprinkle of cocoa powder.

**Variations:**

Use marshmallow topping instead of the chocolate sauce.

# Crème de Menthe Parfait

3 (2-oz.) scoops peppermint
ice cream

6 TB. crème de menthe sauce

3 TB. whipped cream

1 TB. chocolate shavings

| **Yield:** 1 parfait |
| :---: |
| **Prep time:** 3 minutes |
| **Cook time:** None |

1. In a tall glass place 1 scoop peppermint ice cream, and then
   pour 2 tablespoons crème de
   menthe over ice cream.

2. Repeat this process two more
   times.

3. Keep in the freezer until just
   before serving.

4. Top with whipped cream and
   chocolate shavings.

**Variations:**

Alternate crème de menthe with chocolate sauce.

# Chocolate-Covered Coconut Ice Cream Parfait

3 (2-oz.) scoops coconut ice
cream

6 TB. chocolate sauce

3 TB. whipped cream

2 TB. chocolate mint coconut
candy bar

| **Yield:** 1 parfait |
| :---: |
| **Prep time:** 3 minutes |
| **Cook time:** None |

1. In a tall glass place 1 scoop
   coconut ice cream, and then
   pour 1 tablespoon chocolate
   sauce over ice cream.

2. Repeat this process two more
   times.

3. Keep in the freezer until just
   before serving.

4. Top with whipped cream and
   broken pieces of a chocolate
   mint coconut candy bar.

# Cookie Ice Cream Sandwich

2 cookies (about 3 to 3½ inches across)

1 (5-oz.) medium scoop ice cream (softened)

**Yield:** 1 cookie sandwich

**Prep time:** 5 minutes

**Cook time:** None

1. Place 1 cookie right side down on a flat surface.

2. Place a medium scoop softened ice cream on cookie.

3. Place the bottom of second cookie on top of ice cream.

4. Using the flat of your hand, press the top cookie down. This should move the ice cream to the sides of the cookies.

5. Take a butter knife and go around the edge of the two cookies to smooth the edges. Wrap in plastic wrap and place in the freezer for at least a half hour.

### The Real Scoop

With a dozen cookies and 1 quart of ice cream you can get six 5-oz. ice cream sandwiches. (Of course, you can put more ice cream into your sandwiches.)

**Variations:**

Chocolate chip cookies and oatmeal cookies are the ones I like the best.

Chocolate cookies with orange ice cream or orange sherbet.

Any of the Pepperidge Farm cookies are great with this recipe.

My daughter has even used graham cracker cookies.

# Ginger Peach Ice Cream Sandwich

2 ginger or ginger snap cookies
(3 ½ inches across)

1 (5-oz.) scoops peach ice cream

**Yield:** 1 ice cream cookie

**Prep time:** 5 minutes

**Cook time:** None

1. Place 1 cookie right side down on a flat surface.

2. Place scoop of softened ice cream on cookie.

3. Place the bottom of second cookie on top of ice cream.

4. Using the flat of your hand, press the top cookie down. This should move the ice cream to the sides of the cookies.

5. Take a butter knife and go around the edge of the two cookies to smooth the edges. Wrap in plastic wrap and place in the freezer for at least a half hour.

**Variations:**

Place 1 sugar cookie in a plastic bag, and with a rolling pin, make fine crumbs out of it. Now take the ice cream sandwich and roll the side of the cookie with the ice cream into the crumbs.

# Strawberry Ice Cream Sandwich

2 sugar cookies

1 (5-oz.) scoop strawberry ice cream

| |
|---|
| **Yield:** 1 ice cream cookie |
| **Prep time:** 5 minutes |
| **Cook time:** None |

1. Place 1 cookie right side down on a flat surface.

2. Place scoop of softened ice cream on the cookie.

3. Place the bottom of second cookie on top of ice cream.

4. Using the flat of your hand, press the top cookie down. This should move the ice cream to the sides of the cookies.

5. Take a butter knife and go around the edge of the two cookies to smooth the edges. Wrap in plastic wrap and place in the freezer for at least a half hour.

# Brownie Ice Cream Sandwich

1 box brownie mix

1 pt. ice cream

**Yield:** Depends on how you cut the brownies

**Prep time:** 25 minutes

**Cook time:** Follow package directions

1. Follow the directions for heating the oven.

2. Follow the directions for making dense brownies.

3. Butter and flour two 8×8-inch baking pans lined with a piece of waxed paper.

4. Pour batter into pans and bake following the package directions.

5. Remove from heat and cool. When cool, carefully remove brownie from one of the pans, taking care not to break it.

6. Leaving the other brownie in the pan, smooth the pint of ice cream over the top evenly. Place other brownie on top and gently push down.

7. Return to freezer for a half hour.

8. Remove from freezer and cut brownie into as many pieces as you like, and then return to the freezer until a few minutes before serving.

**Variations:**

You can eat as a sandwich or place on a plate and pour a topping over the brownie. Hot fudge is one of my favorites, with a few raspberries placed on top.

Try using chocolate donuts, cut them in half, and scoop ice cream in between the halves. Here again, just add a topping and you have a quick dessert, or place in your freezer and serve as a sandwich.

# Making Your Own Waffle Cone

## In This Chapter

- ☺ How the cone came to be
- ☺ Waffle cone recipes

Okay, I've shown you how to make lots of different kinds of ice cream. But for many people, that's only half the job. A lot of diehard ice cream fans believe there's no other way to enjoy ice cream than in a good old-fashioned waffle cone. So naturally, I want to show you how to be the true ice cream master and make your own cone.

## Cone History

History tells us that paper and metal cones were used in the 1800s in France and Great Britain as an aid in eating ice cream. In England around the same time, people used what was called a penny lick to dispense ice cream. It was a glass cone-shaped dish that looked more like a whiskey shot glass. People would lick the ice cream out of the glass and hand it back for further use. Kind of unsanitary, if you ask me.

In Chapter 1, I told you how a vendor at the 1904 St. Louis World Expo is generally credited with inventing the first waffle cone. There are other people who have also claimed credit for creating the cone, so it's not exactly clear who actually holds that distinction.

Whatever the case, by the mid-1920s the ice cream cone industry was producing 250 million cones a year. Even in a relatively small business like my shop, Four Seas Ice Cream, they use quite a few cones—132,000 in a four-month period during 2004.

# Cones Today

In recent years, more and more homemade ice cream shops are making their own cones on a waffle iron. These cones are larger and hold more ice cream, therefore they are more profitable than the traditional biscuit cone. The smell of these cooking nearby is enough to entice most folks to upgrade their purchase.

### Avoid a Meltdown

You may choose to purchase your cones, but the ones you bake in your own kitchen will surely taste better. To make things really easy, you can purchase a complete waffle-making kit. At the very least, it definitely would be helpful to get a wooden or metal roller, which is shaped like a cone and is sold in kitchenware shops.

# Cone Recipe

1 cup sugar

1 egg

2 TB. melted butter

1 tsp. vanilla extract

¼ cup whole milk

½ cup flour

**Yield:** 8 to 10 cones

**Prep time:** 15 minutes

**Cook time:** 20 minutes

1. Preheat oven to 300°F.

2. In a mixing bowl beat egg with sugar until thick and creamy.

3. Add butter and vanilla and mix well.

4. Slowly add in flour until incorporated.

5. Grease a large cookie sheet and drop 1½ to 2 tablespoons mixture onto the cookie sheet and swirl mixture into a 5-inch circle. Keep circles at least 1 inch apart.

6. Bake for 12 to 15 minutes or until golden brown. Remove from oven and quickly wrap wafer around a cone-shaped mold.

7. Do the same with the rest of the mixture.

### The Real Scoop

Ice cream cones are sold in many different flavors including almond, cinnamon, all fruits, chocolate chip, peanut butter, oatmeal, and even pretzel, but as a person with longevity in the ice cream business, I feel that the quality of the ice cream is far more important than what it sits in.

# Waffle Cones (using a round waffle iron)

2 eggs

¾ cup table sugar

⅔ cup butter melted

1 TB. vanilla extract

¾ cup flour

1. Beat eggs and sugar together until thick and creamy. Add melted butter and vanilla and mix well.

2. Slowly stir in flour until incorporated.

3. Spray the waffle iron with a cooking spray so mixture won't stick.

4. Spoon about 2 tablespoons mixture onto the surface of the waffle iron and spread.

5. Cook until edges are golden brown and not loose in the middle.

6. Remove from iron and wrap around a cone mold.

 **Cool Tips**

There are various companies that sell waffle cone mix and/or waffle cone makers. One place to try is Rival Products (1-800-557-4825).

# Chapter 18

# Ready for a Party?

## In This Chapter

- ○ Popular party desserts
- ○ Secrets to great ice cream pies and cakes
- ○ Making a great Baked Alaska
- ○ Using ice cream molds

Now that you've become an old pro at making ice cream, it's time to celebrate! And what better way to do that than by having a party? Ice cream and other frozen desserts are party staples—in my opinion, they're an absolute necessity for a good party.

I believe that ice cream needs no special ornamentation to be the very best dessert, but for parties and special occasions, something a little more elaborate might be wanted. Presentation is a large part of creating eye appeal. Chefs swirl sauces on ice cream and create landscapes to fit the party theme. Tiny scoops of sorbet can be mixed with fruit or flowers; edible baskets made from shaped biscuits and cookies can be part of an ice cream display. At home you will probably want to stick with ice cream pies, cakes, cookies, or maybe a Baked Alaska.

# Ice Cream Pies

Mixing ice cream with baked goods probably started with America's favorite pie à la mode. Over the years ice cream pies and ice cream cakes have become more popular, and it would be hard to tell which is sold or eaten more. Both items are frequent choices at home, as they can be made with ingredients that most people have in their kitchens and from recipes that people can use for many other desserts.

Let's start with ice cream pies. To make an ice cream pie, all you need is ice cream and a pie crust. Simple, isn't it?

Now decide what flavor of ice cream pie you want to make, and either make or purchase the ice cream. The same with the pie crust: either purchase your pie crust or use one of the following recipes to make it.

# Ice Cream Cakes

Ice cream cakes are very special treats that go so well with birthdays, weddings, anniversaries, holidays, and any special occasions. True ice cream lovers will often seek out an ice cream shop that makes their cakes with all ice cream, or make their own at home. Store-bought angel food cakes or sponge cakes are another choice. In your kitchen, the easiest way to make an ice cream cake is to bake the cake of your choice and, using a springform pan, place a layer of ice cream between the layers of cake.

### Cool Tips

You don't even have to make the cake from scratch; you can purchase a cake mix, bake it, and turn it into an ice cream cake. Frosting the cake is easy, too: Just cover it with whipped cream after freezing and it's ready to serve. Of course, if you like, you can make your own frosting, or buy it in a can.

You must not forget the sauces, either on top or between the layers. Make a two-layer strawberry cake, and place strawberry ice cream and strawberry sauce on the bottom layer. Then repeat the process for the second layer, freeze it, and frost it with whipped cream and whole strawberries. Talk about compliments, your family will be delighted. Hot fudge, caramel, pie fillings, jellies, preserves, or just about anything that can be spread can be used in making ice cream cakes.

I've talked about layers, but that isn't the only way to make an ice cream cake. Another way is to bake a cake, hollow out the middle, fill it with ice cream, freeze, and then frost. This way, you don't have to use a springform pan. You can also hollow out cupcakes and fill with ice cream. Use your best cupcake recipe and bake. Let them cool and then cut the tops of the cupcakes off and hollow out the middle, fill with ice cream, replace the tops, and freeze.

### The Real Scoop

In my family, ice cream cakes were served at two of my children's weddings. Both of the cakes were made by my son Douglas. When Doug's sister Janice married, a 4-foot-high ice cream wedding cake was served. The inside contained 12 different flavors of ice cream. Of course, we have the storage and deep freezers at our shop to be able to make this kind of cake. At Doug's wedding, in all the confusion, someone forgot to temper (let soften) the cake. I don't even think a chain saw could have cut that cake. By the way, that was the last time we ever made an ice cream wedding cake. At Michael and Jennifer's weddings we just served the ice cream with the cake.

# Baked Alaska

Can you imagine placing ice cream in a 450° oven? Well, that's what you will be doing when you whip up some Baked Alaska. You can make this in many shapes, but for the first recipe I am going to use what I believe to be the original bowl shape.

Why doesn't it melt? I've been told that it is the tiny air bubbles in the méringue that insulates the ice cream.

# Using Ice Cream Molds

At one time, it was common practice to use ice cream molds for making special-occasion desserts. Ice cream molds made of pewter have been used for special occasions and banquets for many years. In fact, in the late 1800s and early 1900s they were quite prevalent. They came in all shapes and sizes, ranging from Santa Clauses to locomotives to more simplistic flower and vegetable designs. The molds they used were in great detail (on the inside); when removed, the ice cream was often painted, making a very desirable specialty dessert. It is very difficult to maintain that detail without using dry ice. This is because when you pack a mold with ice cream and place it in your freezer, you must run it under hot water to help release your finished product. The regular deep freeze at 0° to 10° below zero does not get the detail inside cold enough to withstand the hot water release, but dry ice at its much colder temperature works well.

The problem with pewter molds is that they are lead based and there is a small potential danger of lead poisoning.

For home usage, there is no legal problem and many people have used them safely for years. A man from Pennsylvania made a few of a safer metal, but has recently gone out of business. If you wish to purchase or collect the regular pewter molds, simply go to eBay and look under ice cream, as they are available almost daily.

Larger metal and plastic ice cream molds are readily available. A company in New York also makes rubber cake molds (and a few novelty-type molds) for the baking and ice cream industry:

Cold Molds
coldmolds.com
1-800-906-7221

Here's the contact information for a French company that still produces the more ornate molds:

Letang
www.adelphianortheast.com/molds/letang-molds.html

# Basic Graham Cracker Crust Recipe

20 graham cracker squares
(1⅓ cups)

⅓ cup table sugar

7 TB. butter or margarine, melted

| | |
|---|---|
| **Yield:** 1 pie crust | |
| **Prep time:** 20 minutes | |
| **Cook time:** 5 to 10 minutes | |

1. Crush graham crackers into fine crumbs either in a plastic bag with a rolling pin or in a blender. Make about 1⅓ cups of crumbs.

2. Pour crumbs into a mixing bowl and add sugar. Stir until sugar and crumbs are totally combined.

3. Add melted butter or margarine to the crumbs and mix until incorporated.

4. Pour the crumb mixture into a 9-inch pie pan and spread crumbs around the pan evenly. Press firmly onto the bottom of the pie pan and up the sides.

5. Cool pie crust in the refrigerator for about an hour or until it feels firm, or you can bake it in a 350°F oven for 5 to 10 minutes, remove and cool on a rack.

6. While pie crust is cooling, place 1 quart of ice cream (your choice of flavor) in the refrigerator to soften. When soft (but not melted), spread into pie crust shell and cover with plastic wrap. Place in the freezer for about 2 hours. Remove from freezer; slice and serve. (See the sidebar that follows for removing crumb crust from the pan.)

**Variations:**

You can use the same recipe using chocolate graham crackers, low-fat graham crackers, or cornflakes.

### The Real Scoop

How to remove a piece of crumb crust from a pie pan: Wet a towel with very hot water and wring it out well. Rub the bottom and sides of the pie plate with the hot towel. This should soften the butter in the crust, making it easier to remove a slice. You don't have to do this for a baked pie crust.

# Chocolate Cream-Filled Cookie Pie Crust

1¾ cups finely crushed chocolate cream-filled cookies

7 TB. butter or margarine (melted)

| | |
|---|---|
| **Yield:** 1 pie crust | |
| **Prep time:** 20 minutes | |
| **Cook time:** None | |

1. In a mixing bowl combine crushed cookies and melted butter or margarine. Mix until well combined.

2. Pour mixture into a 9-inch pie plate and spread evenly. Press crumbs onto the bottom and up the sides of the pie plate.

3. Cool for about 1 hour in the refrigerator.

4. While pie crust is cooling, place 1 quart ice cream (your choice of flavor) in the refrigerator to soften. When soft (but not melted), spread into pie crust shell and cover with plastic wrap; put into the freezer for about 3 hours.

5. Remove from freezer, slice, and serve. (See the sidebar on the previous page for how to remove crumb crust from the pan.)

**Cool Tips**

You can use any hard cookies with this recipe. Ginger snaps or little round vanilla wafers make a good crust with this recipe.

Now that I have given you a few crust recipes, let's see what you can come up with for filling those pie crusts. Besides adding just the ice cream to your pie shell, you can melt your ice cream and add different ingredients to it, and then pour it into a pie shell. Following are some recipes you might like.

# Peanut Butter Ice Cream Pie

¾ qt. vanilla or French vanilla ice cream (softened)

1 tsp. cinnamon

½ cup crunchy peanut butter

½ cup unsalted peanuts (chopped)

| **Yield:** 1 ice cream pie |
| --- |
| **Prep time:** 20 minutes |
| **Cook time:** None |

1. Allow ice cream to sit in refrigerator to soften.

2. In a mixing bowl combine softened ice cream, peanut butter, and chopped peanuts. Mix until incorporated.

3. Pour mixture into a 9-inch pie crust, cover with plastic wrap, and freeze for at least three hours before serving.

**Variation:**

Use the same recipe, except substitute peanut butter ice cream.

# Easy Lemonade Ice Cream Pie

1 pt. vanilla ice cream (softened)

2 (6-oz.) cans frozen lemonade concentrate (thawed)

8 oz. readymade whipped cream

| **Yield:** 1 ice cream pie |
| --- |
| **Prep time:** 20 minutes |
| **Cook time:** None |

1. In a large mixing bowl, with an electric mixer, mix lemonade concentrate and whipped cream for 30 seconds on low speed.

2. Slowly add in vanilla ice cream and mix until incorporated

3. Pour into a 9-inch pie crust, cover with plastic wrap, and freeze for at least 3 hours before serving.

**Variation:**

Use this same recipe, substituting any concentrate (apple, grape, orange-pineapple, and many more).

# Grasshopper Ice Cream Pie

1 qt. chocolate mint or peppermint ice cream (softened)

8 oz. hot fudge

1 container readymade whipped cream

**Yield:** 1 ice cream pie

**Prep time:** 20 minutes

**Cook time:** None

1. Pour 4 ounces hot fudge into a 9-inch pie crust and spread evenly over the bottom.

2. Pour softened ice cream over hot fudge and spread evenly. Cover with plastic wrap and freeze for at least 3 hours.

3. Remove pie from freezer and drizzle remaining hot fudge over top of ice cream pie. Cover with whipped cream and serve.

# Orange Coconut Sherbet Pie

1 qt. orange sherbet (softened)

6 oz. coconut flakes (chopped fine)

**Yield:** 1 ice cream pie

**Prep time:** 15 minutes

**Cook time:** None

1. Chop coconut flakes until fine. Take 2 ounces and spread over the bottom of a 9-inch pie crust.

2. Spread ½ quart orange sherbet evenly over coconut flakes on bottom of pie crust.

3. Sprinkle another 2 ounces of the coconut flakes evenly over top of sherbet.

4. Spread remaining sherbet over top of coconut flakes and then add rest of coconut flakes to the top.

5. Cover with plastic wrap and freeze for at least 3 hours. Slice and serve.

# Ice Cream Fruit Pie

¾ qt. vanilla ice cream (softened)

2 cups any fresh fruit (strawberries, blueberries, etc.)

Sugar to sweeten

**Yield:** 1 ice cream pie

**Prep time:** 20 minutes

**Cook time:** None

1. Cut and sweeten fruit to taste.

2. Spread half of vanilla ice cream evenly over bottom of a 9-inch pie crust.

3. Spread half fruit mixture over vanilla ice cream.

4. Spread second half of vanilla over fruit and then rest of fruit over ice cream.

5. Cover with plastic wrap and freeze for at least 3 hours. Slice and serve.

**Variation:**

Use the same recipe but with crushed pineapples or sliced peaches. This recipe is made for using your imagination. Don't add the sugar if using sweetened canned fruits.

# Mocha Ice Cream Pie

1 qt. coffee ice cream (softened)

1 cup chocolate sauce

**Yield:** 1 ice cream pie

**Prep time:** 15 minutes

**Cook time:** None

1. Fill a 9-inch pie crust with coffee ice cream and pour chocolate sauce over the top.

2. Cover with plastic wrap and freeze for at least 3 hours. Slice and serve.

**Variation:**

Mix in chocolate chips or crushed nuts.

# Cranberry Sherbet Pie

1 qt. cranberry sherbet

6 oz. chocolate-covered cranberries

**Yield:** 1 ice cream pie

**Prep time:** 15 minutes

**Cook time:** None

1. Fill a 9-inch pie crust with softened cranberry sherbet. Sprinkle chocolate-covered cranberries evenly over top, and gently press into top of sherbet.

2. Cover with plastic wrap and freeze for at least 3 hours. Slice and serve.

**Variation:**

Cut up jelled orange candies and sprinkle over the top when frozen.

# Banana Ice Cream Pie

1 qt. vanilla ice cream (softened)

2 bananas

**Yield:** 1 ice cream pie

**Prep time:** 20 minutes

**Cook time:** None

1. Slice bananas into rounds and line the bottom of a 9-inch pie crust with slices of 1 banana.

2. Pour vanilla ice cream over banana slices and spread evenly.

3. Place remaining banana slices on top of vanilla ice cream.

4. Cover with plastic wrap and freeze for at least 3 hours. Slice and serve.

**Variations:**

Drizzle chocolate sauce over the frozen pie. Or how about a mixture of bananas and strawberries following the same recipe?

# Caramel Ice Cream Pie

1 qt. vanilla ice cream (softened)

8 oz. caramel sauce

| | |
|---|---|
| **Yield:** 1 ice cream pie | |
| **Prep time:** 15 minutes | |
| **Cook time:** None | |

1. Spread softened vanilla ice cream into a 9-inch pie crust.

2. Drizzle caramel sauce over top of ice cream.

3. Using a butter knife, make cross marks in ice cream without touching bottom of pie crust. It should look like caramel streaks in the vanilla ice cream.

4. Cover with plastic wrap and freeze for at least 3 hours. Slice and serve.

# Strawberry Ice Cream Angel Food Cake

3 pt. strawberry ice cream
(softened)

1 (10-inch) angel food cake

1 large container whipped cream
(vanilla or strawberry)

**Yield:** 6 to 10 slices

**Prep time:** 25 minutes

**Cook time:** None

1. Place angel food cake on a flat surface, and with a sharp knife, cut a trench in between the two sides of cake all the way around. Try not to cut through sides or bottom of cake. You should have about ½ inch to ¾ inch edges around cake. (Save cut-out cake pieces.)

2. Spoon softened ice cream into cake trench and compact ice cream without bulging the sides out. Take cut-out cake and fill in top of cake with it.

3. Frost cake with whipped cream and place in the freezer for about 20 minutes. Remove from the freezer and loosely wrap cake or put it in a freezer storage box big enough to hold cake. Freeze for at least another 1 hour before serving. Remember to give cake time to temper before serving, about 10 minutes. Slice and serve.

**Variations:**

This same recipe can be used with any kind of ice cream of your choosing. You can make a butter frosting and use instead of whipped cream. Or just pour one of your favorite sauces or toppings so that it drips over the sides.

# Peach Ice Cream Cake

1 box cake mix (any kind that will complement peaches)

1 cup chopped pecans

6 canned peach halves

1 pt. butter pecan ice cream

4 TB. caramel topping (optional)

| **Yield:** 6 to 10 slices |
| :---: |
| **Prep time:** 20 minutes |
| **Cook time:** Boxed cake cook time |

1. Following the directions for cake mix, add in chopped pecans, and bake in an 11×4½ × 2¾-inch pan according to box's instructions.

2. Follow directions for removing cake from pan and allow to cool thoroughly.

3. Place bottom side up on a serving plate, and cover with ¼ inch whipped cream (optional). Place peach halves evenly around the top of the cake.

4. Using a small scoop, place 1 scoop butter pecan ice cream in each peach hollow. Drizzle warm caramel topping over each half peach and ice cream. Slice at once.

**Variations:**

Use this recipe with pear halves and pear sherbet or sorbet, pouring a little raspberry sauce over the top. Or how about covering the top with a layer of circle-cut bananas and drizzling hot fudge over them?

# Mocha Ice Cream Cake

9-inch springform pan

1 pt. chocolate ice cream (softened)

1 pt. coffee ice cream (softened)

3 TB. crème de cocoa or amaretto (optional)

3 TB. hot fudge (optional)

½ cup finely chopped nuts (your choice)

| | |
|---|---|
| **Yield:** 6 to 10 slices | |
| **Prep time:** 1 hour | |
| **Cook time:** 15 minutes | |

1. Mix up crumb pie crust (recipe given earlier in this chapter). Set aside ⅔ of crumb recipe.

2. Press ⅓ of crumb recipe into bottom of a springform pan and bake in the oven at 350°F for about 15 minutes. Remove from the oven and cool completely.

3. When pie crust is cool, place the pint of softened coffee ice cream into bottom of the springform pan. Pour 3 tablespoons liqueur or hot fudge evenly over top of coffee ice cream, and with a butter knife make cross marks through ice cream. Do not touch the bottom crust. Smooth the top. Place back in the freezer for about a half hour if coffee ice cream becomes too soft.

4. Spread softened chocolate ice cream over top of coffee ice cream and try to keep the top level. Sprinkle remaining crumb recipe evenly over top. Return to freezer for a half hour.

5. Remove from freezer and wipe the sides of the springform pan with a warm, damp towel to release the sides. Remove the side.

6. Using finely chopped nuts, carefully press them into side of ice cream cake all the way around. Return to freezer for at least 2 hours. Slice and serve.

**Variations:**

Here again you can choose any flavor ice cream, liqueur, and/or toppings.

# Ice Cream Pound Cake

1 homemade or purchased
7-inch pound cake

1 qt. ice cream, any flavor
(softened)

1 cup chopped walnuts, or other
nuts

2 (12-oz.) jars preserves (any
that complement ice cream)

**Yield:** 6 to 10 slices

**Prep time:** 1 hour

**Cook time:** None

1. Remove pound cake from container and place in freezer for about 20 minutes.

2. Remove cake from freezer and turn on its side. Cut cake into 3 even slices.

3. Place bottom slice back into container and spread preserves evenly over bottom layer to about ⅛-inch thick. Add ⅓ quart of ice cream evenly over top. Return to freezer for ten minutes.

4. Using second slice of pound cake, spread an even ⅛-inch layer of preserves. Take the previously made layer out of the freezer and place this layer on top preserves side down. Add a second ⅓ quart of ice cream evenly over the top. Again place in freezer for 10 minutes.

5. Take third pound cake layer and spread remaining preserves in ⅛-inch even layer. Remove cake from freezer and place this layer over previous two preserves side down. Top with remaining ⅓ quart of ice cream and sprinkle nuts over ice cream.

6. Return to freezer for a least 1 hour.

7. To remove cake from pan, wet a towel with hot water and wring out. Wrap around pan for a few seconds and, using a knife to loosen the sides, it should come right out on its side. Place upright on a serving plate and slice with a knife wiped with a warm towel.

**Variations:**

Use a chocolate pound cake, or, instead of preserves, use jams or jellies. I have used canned pie filling and strained canned fruits.

# Ice Cream Cake of Many Colors

1 store-bought or homemade
angel food cake

1 pt. cranberry sherbet

1 pt. lime sherbet

1 pt. orange sherbet

**Yield:** 6 to 10 slices

**Prep time:** 30 minutes

**Cook time:** None

1. Remove angel food cake from pan; clean the pan and set aside.

2. Cut angel food cake evenly into 4 layers (horizontally).

3. Place bottom layer of angel food cake back into the clean cake pan and spoon cranberry sherbet on top to about ½ inch thick.

4. Set the next slice from bottom into the cake pan and press gently to secure. Spoon lime sherbet evenly on top of pound cake to about ½ inch thick.

5. Take third slice of cake and place into cake pan over lime sherbet, and press gently to secure. Spoon orange sherbet evenly on top of cake to about ½ inch thick.

6. Place last slice of angel food cake on top of orange sherbet and press gently to secure. Place in freezer for at least 2 hours. Slice and serve.

To release cake and ice cream from the pan, fill a bowl bigger than the cake pan with hot water and set cake pan into it for 2 or 3 seconds. Place a serving dish over the top of cake pan and flip over. If it doesn't release, dip it in the hot water again. When cake is released from the pan, some of the sherbet will be melted and will run down the sides, which makes for a pretty presentation, so be sure your serving place can handle this.

**Variations:**

Use any flavors of sherbet or sorbet with this recipe. I tried it once with ice cream but prefer it with the sherbets.

# Mini Ice Cream Cakes

8 cupcakes, homemade or purchased, with or without frosting

1 pt. favorite ice cream flavor

| | |
|---|---|
| **Yield:** 8 servings | |
| **Prep time:** 40 minutes | |
| **Cook time:** None | |

1. Using a sharp knife, cut off top of cupcake as close to the top as possible. If cupcakes have bottom wrappers, leave them on.

2. Scoop out center in bottom of cupcake, being very careful not to break through the sides. A melon scoop can be used to do this.

3. With a spoon, fill in the hole with ice cream, pressing gently. Place top of cupcake back on, and place in the freezer for at least a half hour.

4. Remove from freezer and quickly frost to your liking.

The last time I used this recipe for the grandchildren, I purchased the cupcakes from the grocery store already frosted. When serving children, I like to leave the paper on, but for adults I remove the paper and serve with a fork or spoon.

**Variations:**

Along with the ice cream filling in the center, you can place candies as a surprise. I also like to take the scooped-out cupcake crumbs and toast them in the oven for about 15 minutes at 350°F, and serve the mini ice cream cakes with a very small side of ice cream with the crumbs over the top. You can also save them for another day. How about trying a chocolate muffin filled with chocolate ice cream with a spoonful of hot fudge poured over the top? Yum.

# Baked Alaska

1 (9-inch) yellow layer cake mix

1 qt. vanilla ice cream

8 egg whites

1 cup table sugar

⅛ tsp. cream of tartar

**Yield:** 6 to 10 slices

**Prep time:** 25 minutes

**Cook time:** Boxed cake baking time

1. Cut heavy brown paper to ½ inch larger than layer cake.

2. Bake layer cake in 9-inch cake pan according to the package's directions or using your own recipe.

3. Remove cooled layer cake from pan and place in center of the heavy brown paper. Place the paper in center of a cookie sheet. Cover with plastic wrap and place in the freezer until needed.

4. Line the 1½-quart mixing bowl with plastic wrap, and spoon vanilla ice cream into it. Place another piece of plastic over top, and press down on ice cream until it is compacted and the top is flat. Place in the freezer until hardened.

5. Take cake and ice cream out of the freezer. Remove ice cream from bowl with the help of the plastic wrap, and place flat side down in center of layer cake. Cover with plastic wrap and return to the freezer.

For the méringue topping:

6. Heat oven to 450°F.

7. Using an electric mixer beat egg whites and cream of tartar until stiff peaks form. Slowly add in sugar a little at a time until stiff and shiny.

8. Retrieve ice cream cake from freezer and completely cover with méringue, forming little peaks all over the surface.

9. Place in the oven for 4 or 5 minutes.

10. Slice and serve immediately.

### The Real Scoop

To make a Baked Alaska, you will need to use a 9-inch cake pan and a mixing bowl that is 1½ quarts in size. You will also need heavy brown paper (a brown grocery bag will do) and a cookie sheet.

# Tiny Baked Alaska

6 1- to 4-inch cookie or cake-type
dessert shells

1 qt. any flavor ice cream

Méringue topping

| **Yield:** 6 servings |
| :---: |
| **Prep time:** 30 minutes |
| **Cook time:** 4 minutes |

1. Place large scoop ice cream on top of cookies. Cover with plastic wrap and place in freezer until méringue is made.

2. Heat oven to 450°F.

3. Use the previous recipe for making méringue. You may have to adjust the recipe to use more or less egg whites.

4. Remove ice cream-covered cookies from the freezer and completely cover ice cream with meringue, making little peaks all around.

5. Place in a preheated oven for three to four minutes or until peaks are browned. Serve immediately.

### Cool Tips

These are fun to make using the leftover egg whites from making your own ice cream.

Part **6**

# Drinks

Some of my favorite ice cream creations don't require a cone or bowl—but rather a cup and a straw. In these last few chapters, I'll discuss ice cream drinks. First I'll show you how to make a bunch of refreshing ice cream sodas. Then I'll walk you through the process of creating the most delicious milk shakes. Finally, I'll share some recipes for floats and other specialty drinks.

# Chapter 19

# Ice Cream Sodas

## In This Chapter

- History of the ice cream soda
- Getting more creative with flavors
- The basic ice cream soda

The corner drug store soda fountain will forever be remembered as a place for families to go and for teenage groups to gather and sip their favorite ice cream sodas. I have special memories of the times spent during my teen and pre-teen years in my small hometown's Central Soda Shop. The most popular item then, and for many years before and after that era, was the ice cream soda. And that is the sole subject of this chapter.

## Ice Cream Soda History

Robert M. Green is credited by most as the inventor of the ice cream soda when he was on hand to celebrate the fiftieth anniversary of the Franklin Institute in 1874. He was a concessionaire who sold soda fountain drinks. The drink he sold was made of sweet cream, syrup, and carbonated water; but he ran out of cream. By substituting some vanilla ice cream, he created the ice cream soda. In fact, it was so successful that he went from averaging $6.00 a day to $600.00 a day. By 1893 the soda was deemed the "National Beverage."

The term "soda jerk" comes from the action of pulling (jerking) the bobtail soda fountain arm forward to stir the syrup and cream in the bottom of the soda glass. After the soda water and ice cream are added, the soda arm is "jerked" forward again to add fizz and foam to the top of the soda.

At the old soda fountains the counter clerk would shout orders to the soda jerks. Here are some of the fun terms used in the good old days:

Adam's Ale—water

Burn it and let it swim—ice cream float

Chicago—pineapple ice cream soda

Chocin—chocolate ice cream soda

Cold spot—glass of iced tea

Cow juice—milk

Draw one—cup of coffee

Eighty one—glass of water

Eighty seven and a half—attractive female approaching

Fifty five—root beer

Freeze one—chocolate frosted

In the hay—strawberry milk shake

One all the way—chocolate soda with chocolate ice cream

Twist it, choke it, and make it cackle—chocolate malted with egg

# Flavor Combinations

Early on, the flavor of the ice cream was usually matched with the same flavor syrup—chocolate with chocolate, etc.—but variety and innovation soon took over. When I started as a soda jerk in 1956, at the shop that I eventually purchased, I took great pride in thinking up flavor combinations. It was a skill that came in handy—at that time; at least 50 percent of the people at the fountain would order an ice cream soda.

I loved thinking up new combinations, recommending different choices to the patrons, and feeling that I was the best soda jerk around.

I'm listing some great ideas in this chapter, but my favorites are chocolate soda with peppermint stick ice cream, lemon soda with lemon crisp ice cream, and chocolate soda with orange sherbet.

Today I still sell a lot of ice cream sodas in their 14-ounce tall glasses, but over the years their popularity has diminished, and sundaes with mix-ins, and milk shakes, have gradually become favorites. This is an art form that is disappearing from the ice cream shops. The problem seems to be that so many shops don't know how to make an ice cream soda properly and that they don't have cold soda water that runs through refrigeration and a carbonating machine that creates soda water. Most soda water today comes from a bottle.

Here are some other ice cream soda suggestions, with the old standbys listed first. Just use the ice cream soda recipe and mix and match.

> **Avoid a Meltdown**
>
> When syrups are not available, you can use sauces, toppings, and fruit preserves as substitutes. It is best to thin them a little with corn syrup or simple syrup.

- ☺ Vanilla syrup with vanilla ice cream (still the most popular)
- ☺ Chocolate syrup with chocolate ice cream
- ☺ Strawberry syrup with strawberry ice cream

And here are some soda combinations:

- ☺ Black and White: chocolate syrup with vanilla ice cream
- ☺ White and Black: vanilla syrup with chocolate ice cream
- ☺ Coffee: coffee syrup with coffee ice cream
- ☺ Mocha: half coffee and half chocolate syrup, with half coffee and half chocolate ice cream
- ☺ Black Cow: chocolate syrup, root beer, and vanilla ice cream
- ☺ Chocolate/Mint: Chocolate syrup with peppermint or mint chip ice cream

- Chocolate/Butternut: chocolate syrup with butter pecan ice cream
- Chocolate/Orange: chocolate syrup with orange ice cream or orange sherbet
- Orange/Chocolate: frozen orange concentrate with chocolate ice cream
- Vanilla/Coffee: vanilla syrup with coffee ice cream
- Coffee/Vanilla: coffee syrup with vanilla ice cream
- Caramel: caramel sauce with vanilla ice cream
- Raspberry: raspberry syrup with black raspberry ice cream or sherbet

**The Real Scoop**

You can use most fruit ice creams to make sodas in the same way: peach, coconut, cantaloupe, blueberry, pineapple, cherry, etc.

- Raspberry/Chocolate: raspberry syrup with chocolate ice cream
- Banana: vanilla syrup with banana ice cream
- Lemon/Banana: lemon syrup with banana ice cream
- Pineapple: pineapple sauce or syrup with vanilla or pineapple ice cream

- Peachy Ginger: peach sauce or syrup with ginger ale and vanilla ice cream
- Strawberry/Ginger: strawberry jam with ginger ale and vanilla ice cream

Plus endless other combinations you can dream up yourself!

**Cool Tips**

Here's a great recipe for a Chocolate Ice Cream Soda from my Four Seas Ice Cream Shop: Into a 14 ounce soda glass or a paper soda cup, I put 2 ounces of chocolate and then I stir in 2 ounces of heavy cream. I use the forward spray of soda water from my fountain to mix the soda water and cream together. Next I fill the glass two thirds full with carbonated water, allowing enough space to place the 7 to 8 ounce scoop of ice cream without the soda water running over the top. Then I fill the rest of the glass using the coarse spray of carbonated water to make a pretty foamy top.

# Basic Ice Cream Soda

14 oz. tall glass

2 oz. syrup

2 oz. heavy cream

4 oz. soda water

1 (7 oz.) large scoop ice cream

**Yield:** 1 ice cream soda

**Prep time:** 5 minutes

**Cook time:** None

1. Put 2 ounces of syrup into a 14-ounce tall glass and stir in 2 ounces of heavy cream.

2. Fill the soda glass two thirds full with soda water. (Allow enough space to place the scoop of ice cream without the soda water running over the top.)

3. Place the scoop of ice cream gently into the soda water and add more soda water to finish filling the glass. Serve with a soda spoon and a straw.

Optional: Place dollop of whipped cream on the top.

**Variation:**

Some people like to put another smaller scoop of ice cream on the top edge of the glass. I don't recommend it, because the ice cream needs to mix with the soda water for a proper ice cream soda.

# Chapter 20

# Milk Shakes, Floats, and Malts

## In This Chapter

- The basic milk shake formula
- Different types of floats
- The popularity of the malt

Milk shakes are a key part of the ice cream industry. Combine a base of flavored syrup with milk and ice cream beaten in a blender, and you have a milk shake. In addition to shakes, this chapter will also teach you how to make wonderful floats and malts.

## Milk Shake Lineage

In New England, a milk shake originally meant syrup and milk, beaten a little in a mixer and served. If you wished ice cream in it, you asked for a frappe. Other names that have been used to refer to milk shakes were frosties (which now mean another type of drink), malts, velvets, and cabinets. Rhode Islanders were used

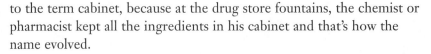

to the term cabinet, because at the drug store fountains, the chemist or pharmacist kept all the ingredients in his cabinet and that's how the name evolved.

Historically, the milk shake is reputed to have been invented in 1922 by a Walgreen's employee, Ivar "Pop" Colson, in Chicago. He simply added two scoops of ice cream into a malted milk drink and mixed the concoction together. Ice cream floats came about in a similar fashion when people decided they had a choice of eating the ice cream ball in the malted drinks with a spoon or to mix it all together.

# All Types of Floats

When you think of floats, you usually think of the sasparalla, root beer, or cola types, but you can float in just about any drink. Try floating on a frappe or a milk shake, but remember to use a taller glass, as the float has a habit of flowing over the top of the glass.

# What's the Story Behind the Malt?

Malt is basically barley or other grain steeped in water until it germinates and then dried in a kiln. It is best known as an ingredient in beer but in ice cream adding malt powder or liquid, especially to chocolate, gives a special, distinct taste.

The malt name became popular nationally because of the chocolate malt powder mixed with milk that Mom was serving to the kids at home. Many times, eggs were added to frappes and shakes for body and taste, along with honey. My personal favorite frappes and milk shakes are made "double thick" with two scoops of ice cream. The long list of combinations would be similar in names to the ice cream sodas (from Chapter 19), so I won't list them again here. You can refer to that chapter if you need help thinking up combinations. Following are just a few more that might just shake up your way of drinking.

## Chocolate Marshmallow Malted Shake

1 cup whole milk

¼ cup marshmallows

¼ cup chocolate syrup

1 TB. malt

| **Yield:** 1 shake |
| --- |
| **Prep time:** 4 minutes |
| **Cook time:** None |

1. Pour milk into blender and add marshmallows, chocolate syrup, and malt. Mix for about 45 seconds

2. Pour into a tall glass and serve.

### The Real Scoop

Thanks to ice cream sodas and milk shakes through the years, the greater gallonage of ice cream has been sold in those mixed drinks than through any other type of service.

## Ginger Pear Shake

2 oz. canned pears or fresh, peeled and sliced

1 cup whole milk

2 oz. ginger ale

| **Yield:** 1 shake |
| --- |
| **Prep time:** 3 minutes |
| **Cook time:** None |

1. If using whole pears, purée them in blender, and then add milk and ginger ale. Blend for about 45 seconds.

2. Pour into a tall glass and serve.

# Grapefruit Shake

6 TB. grapefruit juice concentrate

1 cup whole milk

1 medium scoop vanilla ice cream

| **Yield:** 1 shake |
| --- |
| **Prep time:** 3 minutes |
| **Cook time:** None |

1. Combine juice concentrate, milk, and vanilla ice cream in blender, and blend for 45 seconds. (You can use this recipe for any of the juice concentrates.)

2. Pour into a tall glass and serve.

# Irish Coffee Shake

1 cup whole milk

1 large scoop coffee ice cream

2 TB. whiskey

| **Yield:** 1 shake |
| --- |
| **Prep time:** 3 minutes |
| **Cook time:** None |

1. Place milk, coffee ice cream, and whiskey in blender, and blend for 45 seconds.

2. Pour into a tall glass and serve.

# Prune Shake

3 TB. strained prunes (baby food)
¼ cup orange juice
½ cup whole milk
pinch of salt
1 tsp. lemon juice
1 TB. table sugar
1 (6-oz.) vanilla ice cream

| **Yield:** 1 shake |
| **Prep time:** 3 minutes |
| **Cook time:** None |

1. Mix prunes, orange juice, whole milk, salt, lemon juice, and sugar in a blender, and blend until combined.

2. Add ice cream to blender and beat until blended.

3. Pour into a tall glass and enjoy.

# Coconut Frappe

1 cup whole milk
1 (5-oz.) medium scoop coconut ice cream

| **Yield:** 1 frappe |
| **Prep time:** 4 minutes |
| **Cook time:** None |

1. Place milk and coconut ice cream into blender and mix for 45 seconds. (Blend more or less depending on whether some ice cream chunks or a smooth drink is preferred.)

2. Pour into a tall glass and serve.

# Banana Milk Frappe

1 large scoop banana ice cream or 1
ripe banana, peeled

1 cup whole milk

½ tsp. vanilla extract

**Yield:** 1 frappe

**Prep time:** 3 minutes

**Cook time:** None

1. If using whole banana, place in
   blender and purée; then add
   milk and vanilla, and blend for
   45 seconds. (You can use both
   ice cream and banana for a
   thicker drink.)

2. Pour into a tall glass and serve.

## The Real Scoop

At my ice cream shop, Four Seas Ice Cream, seasoned crew members
have a wonderful time watching the new employees at the shop trying
to make their first frappe on the blenders. I have three of these blenders
and they are set high over the scooping cabinets. There is a knack to
placing the frappe cup on the blender so that the ice cream does not get
stuck on the whipping blades. When this does happen, the ice cream will
throw the milk and syrup up out of the cup and all over the front counter.
It's almost like a rite of passage for the new crew members, but after one
cleanup they soon learn the technique.

# Strawberry Cheesecake Frappe

1 cup whole milk

3 oz. cream cheese

1 large scoop strawberry ice
cream

½ tsp. vanilla extract

**Yield:** 1 frappe

**Prep time:** 4 minutes

**Cook time:** None

1. In a blender combine the milk,
   cream cheese, strawberry ice
   cream, and vanilla extract, and
   blend for 45 seconds.

2. Pour into a tall glass and serve.

# Orange Float

8 oz. orange juice

5 oz. vanilla ice cream

| **Yield:** 1 float |
| --- |
| **Prep time:** 3 minutes |
| **Cook time:** None |

1. Place 8 ounces orange juice in a tall glass

2. Float 5 ounces of vanilla ice cream on top.

# Root Beer Float

8 oz. root beer

5 oz. vanilla ice cream

| **Yield:** 1 float |
| --- |
| **Prep time:** 3 minutes |
| **Cook time:** None |

1. Place 8 ounces root beer in a tall glass

2. Float 5 ounces of vanilla ice cream on top.

**The Real Scoop**

A Root Beer Float is also called a Black Cow.

# Cola Float

8 oz. cola

5 oz. vanilla ice cream

| **Yield:** 1 float |
| --- |
| **Prep time:** 3 minutes |
| **Cook time:** None |

1. Place 8 ounces cola in a tall glass.

2. Float 5 ounces of ice cream on top.

# Purple Cow Float

6 oz. grape juice

2 oz. soda water

5 oz. vanilla ice cream

| **Yield:** 1 float |
| --- |
| **Prep time:** 3 minutes |
| **Cook time:** None |

1. Place 6 ounces grape juice and 2 ounces soda water in a tall glass and mix.

2. Float 5 ounces vanilla ice cream on top.

## Chocolate Peanut Butter Float

6 oz. chocolate milk

2 oz. peanut butter topping

5 oz. chocolate ice cream

| **Yield:** 1 float |
|---|
| **Prep time:** 3 minutes |
| **Cook time:** None |

1. Place 6 ounces chocolate milk and 2 ounces peanut butter topping in a tall glass. Mix well.

2. Add 5 ounces chocolate ice cream on top and serve.

## Lemonade Float

8 oz. lemonade

5 oz. lemon sherbet

| **Yield:** 1 float |
|---|
| **Prep time:** 3 minutes |
| **Cook time:** None |

1. Place 8 ounces lemonade in a tall glass.

2. Add 5 ounces lemon sherbet on top and serve.

# Chapter 21

# Specialty Drinks

## In This Chapter

- ○ How frosteds differ from shakes
- ○ Adding liquor to your frozen drinks
- ○ For the smoothie aficionado

In this chapter I will cover some common specialty drinks, like frosteds, freezes, and a few smoothies. The names and definitions of many of these items are sometimes interchanged, which leads to some confusion in this area.

## Frosteds

Frosteds (freezes) are beaten like a milk shake, but contain no milk—just carbonated water, flavoring, and sherbets or sorbets. To be specific, an orange frosted is orange sherbet and orange carbonated drink placed in a milk shake mixer, beaten until smooth, and then poured into a glass or paper cup. Like most other drinks in this section, they are not as heavy as a milk shake and go especially well on hot days. Frosteds are definitely a precursor to what we call smoothies today. Bear in mind that through the years milk shakes have also been called frosteds.

On hot days, to really help you relax, you will find here a few cold and frosty drinks that contain liquor—only for the big kids. At popular bars many cold liquor drinks are just made with shaved ice, but I feel that ice cream added elevates them to the gourmet category.

## The Real Scoop

At my shop, Four Seas Ice Cream, the favorite frosteds are raspberry, cranberry, lemon, and orange. But then again, those are the only sherbet/sorbet flavors I sell at my shop. I do combine the sherbets and sorbets to make raspberry/lemon frosteds and orange/cranberry frosteds.

# Smoothies

Smoothies have become very popular in the last few years. They are similar to frosteds and freezes, but some are made with soymilk and other healthy products. The recipes that follow are some that I have made at home.

Picture this: It's a hot day and you and the grandchildren have just come home from the beach. It won't be dinnertime for several hours but all you hear is, "I'm hungry." What to do? I get out the blender, open the refrigerator, and make smoothies to stave off the hunger.

The smoothie aficionado says that it is "the fast food" of choice for today's health-conscious lifestyle. Instead of quick hamburgers or candy bars, it is now a smoothie.

The smoothie market has grown by more than 30 percent each year since the late 1990s, and is still growing.

# Four Fruit Frosted

1 cup orange juice

½ cup lime juice

¼ cup lemon juice

1 cup pineapple juice

⅔ cup table sugar

1 pt. vanilla ice cream (softened)

1 qt. soda water

**Yield:** About 6 servings (10 oz. each)

**Prep time:** 15 minutes

**Cook time:** None

1. Mix orange, lime, lemon, and pineapple juices together with sugar until blended well.

2. Add ice cream to juices, and beat until incorporated.

3. Divide mixture into 6- to 10-ounce servings and place in a 16-ounce glass. Add 4 ounces soda water to each individual serving. Stir gently until incorporated.

4. Serve with slice of lemon or orange.

# Grape Berry Orange Frosted

4 oz. orange soda

4 oz. grape drink or juice

1 medium scoop raspberry sherbet (softened)

1 small scoop lime sherbet (softened)

1 small scoop orange sherbet (softened)

12 oz. soda water

**Yield:** About 3 servings (8 oz. each)

**Prep time:** 15 minutes

**Cook time:** None

1. Place orange soda, grape drink, raspberry sherbet, lime sherbet, and orange sherbet in blender, and blend until smooth.

2. Divide mixture into 3 servings, 8 ounces each, and place in 12-ounce glasses. Add 4 ounces of soda water to each, and stir gently until incorporated.

3. Serve with a slice of orange.

## Cherry Brandy Alexander

½ pt. cherry ice cream (softened)
⅛ cup brandy
¼ cup milk

**Yield:** 3 servings
(6 oz. each)

**Prep time:** 3 minutes

**Cook time:** None

1. In blender combine the cherry ice cream, brandy, and milk. Mix for about 45 seconds.

2. Pour into glasses and serve.

## Brandy Alexander

1½ oz. brandy or cognac
8 oz. vanilla ice cream (softened)

**Yield:** 1 serving (8 oz.)

**Prep time:** 3 minutes

**Cook time:** None

1. In blender combine brandy and ice cream. Mix until smooth.

2. Pour into a glass and serve.

# Irish Cooler

1 oz. whiskey

¼ TB. white crème de menthe

8 oz. vanilla ice cream (softened)

| | |
|---|---|
| **Yield:** 2 servings (5 oz. each) | |
| **Prep time:** 3 minutes | |
| **Cook time:** None | |

1. Combine whiskey, crème de menthe, and ice cream in blender and blend for about 45 seconds.

2. Pour into glasses and serve.

# Grasshopper

2 TB. green or white crème de menthe

8 oz. chocolate ice cream (softened)

| | |
|---|---|
| **Yield:** 2 servings (5 oz. each) | |
| **Prep time:** 3 minutes | |
| **Cook time:** None | |

1. In blender combine crème de menthe and chocolate ice cream until smooth, about 45 seconds.

2. Pour into glasses and serve.

# Fudge Coconut Rum

1 TB. rum

2 tsp. coconut flakes (chopped)

3 oz. coconut ice cream (softened)

6 oz. chocolate ice cream (softened)

> **Yield:** 2 servings (5 oz. each)
>
> **Prep time:** 3 minutes
>
> **Cook time:** None

1. In blender place rum, coconut flakes, and coconut and chocolate ice creams, and blend until smooth, about 45 seconds.

2. Pour into glasses and serve.

# Orange Supreme

16 oz. orange sherbet or orange ice cream (softened)

¼ cup light cream

⅓ cup orange schnapps or liqueur

> **Yield:** 3 servings (6 oz. each)
>
> **Prep time:** 3 minutes
>
> **Cook time:** None

1. Combine orange sherbet or ice cream with light cream and liquor in blender for about 45 seconds until smooth.

2. Pour into glasses and serve.

# Strawberry Smoothie

10 oz. crushed ice

1 cup strawberry ice cream (softened)

6 large ripe strawberries (cut up)

¼ cup lowfat plain yogurt

**Yield:** About 3 servings (8 oz. each)

**Prep time:** 4 minutes

**Cook time:** None

1. Place ice in blender and grind until ice is in very small pieces.

2. Add ice cream, strawberries, and yogurt, and grind again. Use a little low-fat milk if mixture is too thick. Add sugar if too tart.

3. Pour into glasses and serve.

# Pineapple Lime Smoothie

1 cup coconut ice cream (softened)

2 oz. frozen pineapple concentrate (thawed)

1 lime (juiced)

10 oz. crushed ice

**Yield:** About 2 servings (5 oz. each)

**Prep time:** 3 minutes

**Cook time:** None

1. Combine coconut ice cream, pineapple concentrate, and lime juice in blender, and mix for about 45 seconds.

2. Add ice and blend until smooth. Add milk to blender to thin out mixture if too thick. Add sugar if too tart.

3. Pour into glasses and serve.

# Orange Pineapple Smoothie

8 oz. orange sherbet (softened)

2 oz. frozen pineapple concentrate (thawed)

10 oz. crushed ice

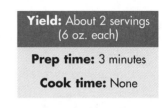

**Yield:** About 2 servings (6 oz. each)

**Prep time:** 3 minutes

**Cook time:** None

1. In blender place orange sherbet and pineapple concentrate, and blend for about 30 seconds.

2. Add crushed ice and mix until smooth. Add milk to blender if mixture is too thick. Add sugar if too tart.

3. Pour into glasses and serve.

# Cider Smoothie

1 cup vanilla ice cream (softened)

2 TB. honey

½ tsp. ground cinnamon

Pinch of ground nutmeg

8 oz. crushed ice

**Yield:** About 2 servings (5 oz. each)

**Prep time:** 3 minutes

**Cook time:** None

1. Place vanilla ice cream, honey, cinnamon, and nutmeg in blender, and blend for 30 seconds.

2. Add crushed ice and blend until smooth. Add milk to blender if mixture is too thick.

3. Pour into glasses and serve.

# Peach Smoothie

3 ripe peaches

1 cup vanilla or peach ice cream (softened)

8 oz. crushed ice

**Yield:** About 3 servings (6 oz. each)

**Prep time:** 3 minutes

**Cook time:** None

1. Peel and pit peaches. Purée in blender.

2. Add softened vanilla or peach ice cream to purée and blend for 30 seconds.

3. Add crushed ice and blend until smooth. Add sugar if too tart.

4. Pour into glasses and serve.

# Glossary

**beat**   To mix with a spoon or mixer until smooth.

**blend**   To mix two or more ingredients together until they are totally combined.

**chill**   To place in refrigerator, cold water, or other cool area until formula is cool throughout. Typically refers to quickly reducing the temperature to 40°F.

**cool**   Not quite as cold as chilled. Generally, cooling is achieved simply by letting the mixture sit at room temperature.

**dash**   A small amount; a few drops.

**dasher**   The paddle inside an ice cream maker.

**dice**   To chop into small pieces or cubes.

**ice bath**   To place bowl of ice cream mixture into larger bowl filled with ice and water.

**ice cream**   A dessert made with a cream base, along with sweetening and flavoring.

**ice cream soda**   A beverage/dessert consisting of ice cream and soda.

**novelty**   A frozen dessert product made in single-serving sizes and packaged separately.

**purée**   To process ingredients in a blender until they achieve a slushy consistency.

**scalding**   The process of heating cream slowly in a saucepan until it has almost reached the boiling point, and then cooling.

**sherbet**   A frozen dessert similar to ice cream, but with less milk or cream.

**simmer**   To cook at low heat without boiling.

**sorbet**   A frozen dessert usually made from fruit juice and/or puréed fruit.

**whip**   To mix more rapidly than beating or stirring.

**zest**   The colored outer layer of peel on a citrus fruit.

# Index

# D